The Lucky One

By

Sherry V. Ostroff

9.99

ISBN-13: 978-1523956210
ISBN-10: 1523956216

Library of Congress Control Number: 2016902812

CreateSpace Independent Publishing Platform, North Charleston, SC

The Lucky One

The Lucky One

By

Sherry V. Ostroff

This book is dedicated to

My grandchildren

Ethan Walker
&
Colin Benjamin

My mother never knew them, but she would
have loved them dearly.

Table of Contents

The Lucky One
Introduction

My earliest cherished memory of my mother was our time spent together while she told me stories. This was when I had her undivided attention, and she demanded mine. Unlike other women of her day, my mother was not a stay-at-home mom. Because of economic necessity, she was forced to go to work full time at McCrory's Five & Dime selling notions when I was five years old. My parents needed the additional income to help fortify a desperate household budget. Therefore, the time we spent together was precious, so no distractions were permitted.

No matter what story my mother chose to relate, whether it was her very different and difficult childhood or her favorite novel, it became an opportunity for us to be together. Like a great riveting book it provided a brief escape from reality. It was not only a diversion for me but for my mother as well.

I can remember clearly how it all began. My mother started me off with Bible stories. While some children learned about Old Testament characters and events from Little Golden Books or attending Sunday school, I learned about our forefathers and foremothers in a cozy setting, my mother's kitchen. My young mind tried to wrap itself around all the wonders of Joseph and his coat of many colors or of Noah who lived in an ark for forty days in an effort to save humanity and the animals from the flooding waters. But, my favorite of all the stories in the Bible was Moses and the Ten Commandments. My mother's telling of these stories mingled with the many aromas of her cooking. From her chicken soup simmering away in the big metal pot or the sweetness of her rice keegel, to the browning of Fayge's cookies in the oven, it was all divine. The food, the aroma, and my mother's stories, will always be a part of my childhood.

In my mother's tiny kitchen we could not help but to be close. It was barely four by six feet, and within that space there was a four burner gas stove and oven, a refrigerator, a white enamel sink, a few wooden cabinets and a small Formica table with four metal chairs. We barely had any room to move so closeness was a given. While she rolled the dough for varenikis (pierogis, Russian style) or as she amazingly skinned an apple in one long unbroken peel my mother could make Moses, the Deliverer, come alive for me. It was as if I walked beside him as he defied Pharaoh's anger and rained havoc on the Egyptians. I stood on the shores of the Red Sea and watched Moses raise his shepherd's staff to part the waters, and I bore witness when he destroyed the Ten Commandments as punishment to the idol worshipping Israelites. I was transported to another time and place, and I was no longer in that tiny kitchen. The walls melted away and I effortlessly traveled back in time with my mother's voice as my guide.

Storytelling was a way for my mother to share the knowledge she gained from her reading. She would choose books and characters that would demonstrate moral and ethical behavior so that I would learn right from wrong. She never completed her high school education because of the Depression and her obligation to her family, but that did not matter. Not having a diploma, she believed, was a poor excuse to forgo one's self-education through reading. Therefore, to my mother, there was nothing more precious than a great well-written book and each one that she chose to tell me about had to include an important message. If a book could not offer something of value, something worthy to take away from, then what was the point of wasting your time turning pages. As a result, comic books and many contemporary novels were never allowed in her home, or in my hands.

My mother's home was filled with books owned and loaned. The few she owned outright had an honored and cherished place in the top half of a glass enclosed secretary in the living room. Her library had all of the classics including *Ivanhoe, Robinson Crusoe, The Last of the Mohicans* and plays by Shakespeare. My mother also had a worn-out copy of *Forever Amber* which she perceived as way too scandalous and risqué for my young mind. Those books not encased but piled high on end tables or by her plastic covered chair, were loaners

3

from the public library. The loaners were also treasured and cared for so to be enjoyed by the next reader.

Her favorite book, which she read long before I was born, was Victor Hugo's healthy tome *Les Miserables*. The size of the book never daunted her. She was delighted if a good book was lengthy because she did not want it to end. She also claimed that the best books were thick, and she considered the additional hours needed as time well spent. If there were a lesson to be learned from the book, as in the case of good winning over evil in *Les Miserables*, what did it matter if it took you a while to read. For my mother it was quality versus quantity or was it quantity equaled quality?

I never shared my mother's love of *Les Miserables* except for the musical version. Maybe it was because she was so passionate in her love for the book and pushed hard for me to love it too. She proved how special Hugo's written word was to her when she once had the opportunity to see the Broadway version. She's the only person I know who walked out during the intermission of the hit show. How dare the great master's work be adapted to song and dance. I was speechless when she told me.

Telling a lengthy story was never a problem for my mother, the storyteller. Instead of recounting the tale at one sitting, I would hear it in segments that could go on for weeks. She always knew where she left off, and if I did not remember any preceding part of the book, she would have no trouble summarizing. This was almost a requirement to move forward with a long story. Occasional breaks, like commercials, were allowed in the case of bathroom visits. My mother's method of telling stories was the original episodic television that is so prevalent today. This Scheherazade was way ahead of her time.

Not all of my mother's story telling was based on the classics. Besides the Bible stories which I truly loved, and which ultimately began my journey as a lifelong lover of anything history, I was enraptured with my mother's tales of her childhood. It was so foreign to my own experience which seemed safe, peaceful and uneventful in comparison. When she described her life in Eastern Europe it was as if I was transported to a different time and place, and I, a young child, could meet my mother on equal footing. Besides Moses, it was the one set of stories that I would often request to hear over and over again, and they are the ones that have stayed with me to this day.

As I moved away from my mother's home and created my own I never heard the stories any more. I had a feeling she was telling my daughter some of the same tales when she and my father came to babysit, but since I was absent I never heard them. The time had come for my daughter and my mother to have their special moment together.

It was not until my mother was in her late 60's, shortly after she retired, that I suggested to her that she write down the story of her childhood. There were several reasons that prompted me to ask her at that time in her life. First, she had just recovered from a massive heart attack and subsequently spent thirty days flat on her back in intensive care. There were times I thought she would not survive, and that was a stark reminder that my parent was not meant to last forever, that life is brief and untold stories would vanish. Second, genealogy and searching for information about one's ancestors was made easier by the Internet and this pastime was becoming increasingly popular. I longed to have a more complete story of my mother's childhood and her birth family. Lastly, I realized I had a wonderful primary source in my mother. She lived during a time of great social upheaval and momentous worldwide change, and that along with her personal riveting history was meant to be shared and saved. Coupled with the fact that she was a great storyteller, I knew I had to get her to put it down on paper. Crazily, I thought by suggesting this project to my mother, I was being a good daughter since I was giving her something constructive to do with her leisure time in retirement. I think my mother didn't do it for any of the reasons I thought were important. I believe she did it for the reason that mattered most to her, she loved to tell stories.

I wanted her to describe life in Eastern Europe in the first quarter of the 20th century. I wanted her to relate how it felt to leave the country of her youth and immigrate to the United States. I wanted to know how it was to be a stranger in a strange new land. I wanted to know these things not as a child but now as an adult. I already knew by heart the funny sanitized version meant for a child's ears and imagination. Now I wanted her story full strength, not watered down, no matter how bitter, gruesome or painful.

What I didn't expect was that the storyteller took me seriously and she accepted my proposal immediately. Within a few months my mother handed me a 100 page manuscript. It was written in first person, autobiographical. Thus, it is her voice you hear loud and clear. It was all done by hand because my mother, much to her dismay, never learned touch typing. The handwriting was done in cursive style in pencil and in pen on lined and unlined paper. Much of it is double-sided and each page is numbered. In the case where she wanted to include an addendum, maybe it was something she forgot in the course of her writing, she used a lettering system to correspond with the page. So, while there is a page 40, there is also a page numbered 40A, 40B, and so forth. I knew exactly where the add-on stories were supposed to go.

I don't remember our having much of a discussion when she handed her completed story to me. After all, I thought I knew much of what was written on those pages, or did I? While reading her story I had two reactions. The teacher in me took over, and I started to correct the poor grammar, spelling and misplaced or omitted words. My immigrant mother still struggled with her adopted language.

Storytelling was different this time because now she was committing the tale to the written word rather than the spoken word. My mother wrote as she talked which was partly the source of her difficulty. Part way through my correcting I froze and realized how important it was to allow her to tell her story in her words, broken or not. How dare I try to correct her meaning and perhaps alter it. Luckily, the grammatical and spelling difficulties in no way hindered her unbelievable page-turner of a story. My second thought was her tale had the DNA for a great novel or movie.

About ten years after I received the manuscript my mother's voice was silenced. How lucky it was for me that I asked her while she was still able to remember and have the strength and courage to put it all to print. I have read her story many, many times since, and I realize how fortunate I was to get her story for future generations of my family and for others who never knew her. I have told her amazing tale to extended family, friends and students. Ironically, I have now become the storyteller, and now it is time that I make her voice known and continue her legacy.

Sherry V. Ostroff

Clarification

The following is my mother's story. I have maintained her writing, as much as possible, in her exact words. If a word was omitted, I have used brackets to show my addition; this was done only to improve meaning. Any parenthesis is hers. Punctuation was corrected only when necessary. Spelling has been corrected. Although the grammar is poor, her story is clear.

By limiting the corrections, I wanted the reader to understand the difficulty of mastering the English language for an immigrant, even one who had been in the United States for sixty years at the time of the writing.

All of the original manuscript from my mother is presented in this book in italics. My writing is not in italics.

The italicized story is divided into six chapters which alternate with my chapters of historical detail and background information. The length, topic and title of each chapter were chosen by my mother.

Life in Russia

*All of my mother's family was born in Russia in Keifer Gu Bone [*Kiev Gubernia – an administrative division of the Russian Empire*] which means in the vicinity of Kiev. The vicinity consisted of small villages and small towns. If you mentioned any town or village around that area my mother seemed to have some relative there: a sister, brothers, parents, uncles, aunts, cousins, great aunts, great uncles, nieces and nephews. She always seemed to know the top notch citizens of each village and town and how these families [were] related to them, or how some were friends of them.*

My [maternal] grandfather was a religious man, orthodox and so [was] my grandmother. They lived in Russia for generations and the family was well known in that area, it was a proud and honorable family. My grandparents had five children, three boys and two girl: Mendel, the oldest, my mother Shandel, Ruchel [Etta], her sister, Yolick (Julius) and Moishe the youngest.

My grandfather earned his living by dealing with forests as did many Jews at that time. He would chop up trees and have them imported to his village where he had a lumberyard of his own. He never really put his hands to work. He did only in the business angle of it. He had his own horses and wagons, stables and workers to take care of everything.

11

His house was small but comfortable, he had a maid and a cook. Around his house he had a beautiful well- kept garden, and a gardener. When the gardener had certain dirty work to do, or planting to do, he wore white gloves to protect his hands. Not only were there flowers in the garden, they were beautifully arranged in different designs. Then there were fruit trees, especially rare apple trees of different varieties, which my grandfather brought home from his different travels. Once, [one] of the apple trees became diseased. The gardener treated that tree and saved it, and after it recovered he did not allow anyone to eat its fruit for five years. He ate the first apple and then he allowed the [family] to start eating the fruit again.

My grandfather brought many rare and different things home from his travels, one of which was a rare and very beautiful China Closet. It came in many boxes and it was assembled right in front of your eyes without one single nail or hammer and it could be folded back again in the boxes and then stored away.

All my grandfather's children went to synagogue and Hebrew school. The Hebrew school consisted of one room and the rest of the house was for [the teacher] and his family. The children started Hebrew school when they were very young. They didn't have to go to the Russian schools. It wasn't compulsory. Few Jewish children went to the Russian schools [because they were] not wanted there. They were very expensive and you had

*forever to bribe the officials. Besides that, the
Jewish children were always being ridiculed and at
times beaten, in other words, it was dangerous.
Who went to the Russian schools, not [the]
peasants' children, they were not allowed in, and
also [they] couldn't afford it. The farmer and the
peasant were doomed - he died ignorant. He could
[not] read or write. Any document he had to sign
he signed by just putting down a cross. The king
didn't want him educated.*

*So most of the Jews' education was Jewish
(Yiddish jargon), Hebrew, the Bible, and the
Talmud - which was the philosophy of the sages,
and for some also the Kabala which was the
supernatural which few studied or understood, and
that was studied only by a few people and [at] a
very mature age in their lives. But for most, it was
Jewish, Hebrew, the Bible and the Talmud.*

*So who went to the Russian school? The
upper and middle [class] Russian children, the
landowner's children, the doctor's children, the
officer's children, and the official's children [went].
Some Jewish children did get into high school
through bribery. They learned to speak Russian by
dealing with the peasants. They learned to read
and write the Russian language by a few Jews that
knew how, [or] they taught themselves. They read
as many books as they could lay their hands on.
They kept it a secret from the government and
sometimes also from their parents. When they got
older they would tell their parents, what they had*

13

learned, and if the parents were free thinkers they were glad and if they could afford it, they hired a teacher to come to the house and prepare the youngster to enter (gamaze) high school. Then the bribery started and the danger. If the bribery was discovered the Jew was always at fault, and they had to pay dearly for it.

Well, to get back to the one room Hebrew School, the teacher was usually a well-known person, respected and well-versed in Hebrew and its teachings. There usually was only one fault, he had all this knowledge but he didn't know how to teach, but he gave it all he could and slowly, and with great pain and with an iron hand, he taught his students. His teaching was effective because the children were always under the watchful eyes of the fathers. They had to pray at home daily and at the synagogue. They had to discuss the Talmud with their fathers and the elderly.

The children went to school from early morning till the setting sun. The Russian winters were long and bitter, but the children went in the bitterest cold and (the) deepest snow, but they had their fun on snowy days. They would throw themselves flat on the snow to show their mark. They carried lighted lanterns when it was dark, they sang their Hebrew songs and danced, jumped and sometimes the boys had snow fights.

In the summer they went bathing, boys and girls separated, with their underwear on.

One summer my mother, Shandel, and her brother Yolick (they were close in age) decided to play hooky and not go to Hebrew school. They went bathing in the river instead. They had great fun and thus stayed out of school from Monday till [Thursday]. Friday, they decided to go to the Hebrew school because [on] Friday my grandfather asked his children what they had learned during the week and they better know what that was. So Friday morning my mother and her brother showed up in school. The teacher wanted to know if they had been sick, and they both assured him they were in good health. So the teacher asked my mother first, what was the reason she did [not] show up in school? "Well," said my mother, "it was raining." The teacher, hearing this excuse got a glint in his eyes and went along with the excuse, but he asked the class, "Did it rain all week?" The children replied in chorus, "No, it didn't." My mother very wisely said, "Yes it did rain, just around [my] house."

Another episode my mother told about [school] was that the children sat around the [teacher] on a coarse wooden table on long wooden benches. The teacher had a very bad habit, he wanted to hear each child recite his lesson and would call [the student] over to where he was seated, and made him sit down close to him and recite the lesson. If you didn't do so well he would put his hand under the table and give you a pinch on your leg. Well, Yolick didn't know his lesson one day, and [when] he sat near the teacher he put one of his legs over the little boy sitting next to him. When the teacher put his hand under [the] table he pinched the wrong boy.

Another prank the kids did [was when] the teacher left the room for a few minutes, they would change the time on the clock on the wall. One by [one, they] would bend over and another boy got on his back and change[d] the time.

As the years went by and the children [in the family] grew up, the oldest son Mendel turned out to be very learned and very orthodox. He married well, didn't believe in being fancy or putting on airs, he lived quietly and all of his children were girls. One daughter died in infancy due to a fire. [The] mother left the infant in her [older daughter's] care and [was] told to heat up the milk on the open fire. Her clothes caught on fire. [The older sister survived but the baby did not.] My Aunt Ruchel [Etta], my mother's sister, married a business man and had two boys.

My mother Shandel married into a well-known and respected family from another village. [My paternal grandparents] had a dry good's store. My grandfather from my father's side was well learned, pious and never worked. That was the custom then - the men studied the Bible and the Talmud, the women carried on the business, and they did it gladly. So my grandmother on my father's side tended the dry good's store and she did a very good job too. They were well-to-do and

16

known far and wide in that area and surrounding villages and towns.

My Uncle Yolick married and had one child, a little girl. He left his wife and child and went to America because he did not want to go serve in the Russian army.

My youngest uncle, Moishe, took it in his head he wanted to be a doctor. My grandfather pleaded with him, to be a rabbi but to no avail. He left Russia and went to Romania to study. There he married a head nurse from a hospital. Her family was well respected and her two sisters were druggists, a field that was rare for a woman to be in. They were the ones that I never knew. In Europe, a drug store was a highly respected business. They didn't sell anything but drugs. [There was] no such thing as side merchandise like note books, pencils, or newspapers. The drug stores in Europe really smelled like medicine when you entered them. You sat quietly and waited for the prescription to be made. Sometimes you waited over an hour because they had to mix the drug themselves from scratch. The town my Uncle Moishe lived in was Beltz,[Balti] Bessarabia, Rumania. If you have ever heard the song on records or sung in Jewish houses, " Mayn Shtetle Beltz", well that is one and the same town. I never knew my Uncle Moishe's family.

Ita Pogrebiski

Life in Russia

My mother, Ita Pogrebiski, was born sometime in 1918 near the city of Kiev, in the Russian Pale of Settlement where her family had lived for generations. Ita was her Jewish name, Ducia was her Russian name. My mother never knew the date of her birth. There was no official documentation, no baptism registry, and no family Bible entry. No one, not even her own mother, remembered the day when the youngest of six children entered the world. This was due to the acceptance of an unusual ancient Jewish custom to ignore birthdays because it was a yearly reminder that life was getting shorter. No one in her immediate family discussed birthdays or how old they were. This custom continued for many decades even after my mother's family lived in the United States. When my mother's sister, Aunt Anna, would visit, I was forewarned not to insult her and embarrass my mother by asking Aunt Anna any birthday details. That was a tall order for a young child who was thoroughly Americanized and loved birthdays. Besides, I believed, age defined one's pecking order in life, but I knew when to keep my mouth shut.

Years later when my mother was applying for US citizenship, a birth date was necessary, so she chose the second of March because it was not close to any major holidays. My father always knew the truth, but my mother kept her unknown birth date a secret from me for many years, and it was only towards the end of her life that she shared the information. By then, it did not seem to matter. While her birth date was a mystery, the place where she was born was a well-known fact.

My mother's story begins with her mother, Shandel, a young school girl living with her very religious parents and many siblings in The Pale. She was born in 1887, a fact none of her three surviving children, Hunala, Jack and Ita, knew. When Shandel died in May, 1950, her children listed the year 1900 on her headstone. This was not correct. If that were the case, and based on the information my mother supplied in her memoir, Shandel would have been about three when she had her first child. Additionally, at the Ellis Island Passenger Online Search, Shandel Pogrebiski, housewife, was forty years old at the time of her entry into the United States in 1927. It was a long arduous journey of many years and miles from The Pale.

The Pale of Settlement was a vast territory on the western side of Imperial Russia and as the government annexed more land it eventually encompassed 472,590 square miles from the Baltic to the Black Sea. It included what is today Estonia, Latvia, Lithuania, Belarus, the Ukraine, the Republic of Russia, Moldova, part of Poland and Romania.

The Pale of Settlement got its name from the original meaning of the noun "pale" or "palisade."

A pale was a wooden stake that was hammered into the ground and was meant to define the boundary of a town or conquered land. A single pale could be the start of a fence that would define legal occupancy to either discourage an unwanted population from entering or to maintain the local citizenry within. At times, the boundary became more than a fence, perhaps a barrier like a stone wall, but the intent was the same.

The Russian Pale of Settlement was not the first of its kind. The earliest recorded use of the term "pale" was in fourteenth century Ireland when the English exercised control over Dublin. The boundary for the town was marked with pales. Thus, the area within the markers was called The Pale of Dublin.

At this time the phrase "beyond the pale," came into use. It had political, geographical and social ramifications. If you lived "beyond the pale" then you resided outside the acknowledged jurisdiction of the city or town. Inside the pale was a modicum of safety, law and order, beyond the pale was barbarity and the feared unknown. At least, that was what the powers in charge wanted the masses to believe. No matter how you looked at it, living "beyond the pale" was deemed unwise and unsafe.

The phrase was also used to describe unacceptable behavior. An example of this is in Charles Dicken's book *The Pickwick Papers* published in 1837. "I look upon you, sir, as a man who has placed himself beyond the pale of society, by his most audacious, disgraceful, and abominable public conduct".

The Russians established their Pale in December, 1791. Its creation came about because some tsars tried to expel the Jews who were perceived to be a religious and economic threat. Only Catherine the Great was successful in a way. She viewed The Pale as a compromise between expulsion and placating those threatened by the Jewish menace. Jews were required to live and work in The Pale separating them, as much as possible, from the Russian population.

The event that heightened Russian angst over the Jews had begun two decades earlier. In 1772, the first of three partitions of Poland brought huge numbers of Polish Jews into Imperial Russia. Up until that time, the Russian-Jewish population was miniscule, but with the annexation of Polish territory, Jews became a sizable and therefore threatening minority. In 1772, Poland had the highest concentration of Jews in the world, and now many of them fell under the jurisdiction of the Russian government.

Many of these Polish Jews were merchants and craftsmen and their Russian counterparts, mainly in Moscow, feared this new, unfair competition. Unfair, because it was falsely believed that the Jewish businessmen were dishonest, and therefore unworthy to share the economic pie. What else,

In 1874 the military service exclusion for residency requirement outside The Pale was changed. The twenty-five years of mandatory service was reduced, but only those Jews who served under the old conscription laws of 1827 were allowed to domicile outside The Pale. Also rank or membership in a revered group like the Imperial Guard could relax the rules. This dispensation for military service did not last.

Jews who were registered members of the First Guild, master craftsmen, could live outside of The Pale, but there were restrictions placed on the number of years required for membership. If the Jewish craftsman was a member for less than ten years, he and his family were forced to move back into The Pale. Entrance into the guild, however, was difficult because it required permission from the government. It was a catch-22.

Living inside The Pale did not lessen the restrictions and the exceptions. Cities like Kiev, Nikolaev and Sevastopol were off limits, but again, there were concessions.

With the rise of the French Revolution, Catherine the Great banned any imports from France: wine, perfume, fabrics, jewelry, etc. She didn't want to aid the French economy. However, it was feared that Jewish merchants, deprived of some of their French merchandise or seeing an opportunity to make a profit in the black market, would engage in illegal activities. Therefore, Jews were not permitted to live within fifty miles of the western border for fear they would engage in smuggling. Ironically, Jews were permitted to travel freely within The Pale, something that non-Jewish Russian citizens were denied. With the many conflicting and confusing exclusions and exceptions in place there was one guarantee, the rules were anything but clear.

Still, there were Jews who lived clandestinely outside The Pale until the Russians rounded up the lawbreakers. This was done in Moscow and St. Petersburg. When the illegals were discovered they were returned in chains. This police action, at times, would cause international outrage and internal chaos, so from 1880 to 1893, Jews were allowed to remain outside of The Pale if they had already established residency before a certain date. This was repealed in 1893.

Further restrictions were created as the Jews were scapegoated for events beyond their control. In 1881, Tsar Alexander II was assassinated by the terrorist group *Narodnaya Volya* or People's Will. The bomb thrower was a Catholic Pole but since one of his confederates came from a Jewish family that was enough to blame the entire community and punish them with a series of restrictive laws called the May Laws of 1882. These laws were meant to limit access to education, employment, and areas of residence. Quotas were established for higher education enrollment even though many schools remained partly empty. Jews were banned from taking the bar exam to practice law and there was a sharp reduction in the number of doctors allowed to work in the military. In later years, Jews were banished from Kiev and Moscow which resulted in thousands being forced into The Pale which resulted in American President Benjamin Harrison's public condemnation. Ignoring international outrage, a year later all Jews living in The Pale were banned from voter participation. In 1882 hundreds of shtetls (a small town) were upgraded to villages. Jews were denied access to villages and were forced to move elsewhere. The result was massive overcrowding and unemployment in certain areas of The Pale. The draconian May Laws were only meant to be short-lived, but they endured for thirty-five years.

Another consequence of the assassination of the Tsar was the rise of anti-Jewish riots called pogroms. The death of the Tsar was not the only catalyst of these murderous rampages. Jew-hatred stemmed from the economic hardships of the time as well, and someone had to be blamed. Fanning the flames were the press, the government, the military and the church. All were responsible for the destruction of Jewish lives and homes.

The pogroms and the May Laws were the major reasons for the growth of the Zionist movement (the quest for a Jewish homeland) and the exodus of 2,000,000 Jews between 1881 and 1914 to Great Britain and the United States.

Into this milieu my mother was born. Although The Pale was officially ended in 1917, the restricted life and the danger imposed by the pogroms did not ease up immediately. By this time, most of my mother's uncles had either left Russia or were in the process of doing so. Her teenage sister Hunala (Anna), left for the United States soon after my mother was born. A few years later, her brother Jack followed. First, he fled to Romania and then to the United States.

Some fled because of the required military service which took young boys away from their families and religion for many years until they barely remembered who they were. Others left due to the lack of opportunity resulting from a stifling educational and occupational environment. Others emigrated in pursuit of a better life including the freedom to practice their religion and to speak their mind. In the case of baby Ita and her recently widowed mother, Shandel, they needed to get out of Russia as soon as possible because their lives were in mortal danger from the unrelenting pogroms.

Sherry V. Ostroff

Family Tree:

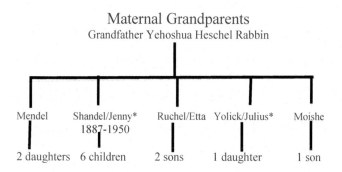

Maternal Grandparents
Grandfather Yehoshua Heschel Rabbin

Mendel	Shandel/Jenny* 1887-1950	Ruchel/Etta	Yolick/Julius*	Moishe
2 daughters	6 children	2 sons	1 daughter	1 son

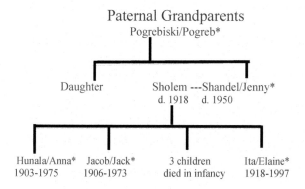

Paternal Grandparents
Pogrebiski/Pogreb*

Daughter   Sholem ---Shandel/Jenny*
             d. 1918   d. 1950

Hunala/Anna* 1903-1975	Jacob/Jack* 1906-1973	3 children died in infancy	Ita/Elaine* 1918-1997

*Named changed after arriving in the United States

29

THE PALE 1835-1917

0 [   ] 200
Miles

1891. 2,000 Jews deported, many of them in chains

1855. Open to Jews
Moscow

1891. 20,000 Jews expelled

St.Petersburg

KOVNO
VITEBSK
VILNA
SUWALKI
PLOCK
LOMZA
GRODNO
MINSK
MOGILEV
WARSAW
KALISZ
SIEDLCE
PIOTRKOW
RADOM
KIELCE
LUBLIN
VOLHYNIA
CHERNIGOV
Brody
Kiev
KIEV
POLTAVA
PODOLIA
EKATERINOSLAV
BESSARABIA
KHERSON
Nikolaev
TAURIDA
Sebastopol
Yalta
Black Sea

GERMANY
AUSTRIA-HUNGARY
RUMANIA
Baltic Sea

Principal town from which in 1880 began the exodus of over two million Jews from the Pale to the United States, Britain, Europe, South America, and Palestine

In 1822 500,000 Jews living in rural areas of the Pale were forced to leave their homes and live in towns or townlets (shtetls) in the Pale. 250,000 Jews living along the western frontier of Russia were also moved into the Pale. 700,000 Jews living east of the Pale were driven into the Pale by 1891

☐ The Pale of Settlement. Russian Jews confined to this area by laws of 1795 and 1835. By 1885 there were over 4 million Jews living in the Pale

⊙ Towns within the Pale barred to Jews without special residence permits

30

My Mother's Wedding

Now that [I] have told you how my mother's brothers and sister grew up and went in different directions as they became adults, I must tell you about my mother's wedding. My [maternal] grandfather's home and business was in a town called Parlicka [sic] in the vicinity of Kiev, and the family was well-known in different towns through [the] business and relations. Not far away was this other town called Zivitov, all in the vicinity of Kiev. Of course, my mother's father also had relatives in Zivitov, and being a prominent person [he] also knew the prominent families in Zivitov. When my mother was little, [her] father and this prominent family made a pact that their son who was a couple of years older would marry my mother when she became of marriageable age. In their early teens they had a glimpse of each other. The appearance of each one was favorable. My mother was considered quite a beauty. My father was of medium height, thin build, brown hair, and looked handsome in his own way. He had a beard which made him look older. Marriageable age meant he was at the most eighteen years old. My mother was fifteen.

My mother didn't exactly want to marry such a religious person but she couldn't object because her own family was just as religious. She resigned herself to this fact and no one knew of her inner desire.

The agreement between the fathers was that in the first two years of their marriage they were to live in their parents' house. The first year they were to live with the groom's parents - rent and food free. If a child came along all medical expenses were paid by the parents. Also if the couple needed medical treatment the parents also paid it. The dowry that my mother's father gave was to go and put the young groom into some kind of business. In the second year the couple, if by then they had offspring, [they were] to live at [my] mother's side [of the] family, same arrangement, rent, food and medical expenses free. That gave the young couple a chance to establish themselves in a business, and if that didn't go well my grandfather on my mother's side was to take the groom into his business.

Thus the first year my father bought this jewelry store of which he didn't know how to run or what to do. The whole venture was a sheer loss. So my grandfather took him in to the lumber business and they did well.

So let's get on with the wedding. The wedding trousseau had long been laid away for, ever since my mother was a small child. There were any number of linens, tablecloths, napkins, kitchen towels for dairy and others for meat, sheets, pillow cases, comforters, pillows, yards and yards of cloth for dresses, yards and yards for under clothes, yards for night clothes, robes and coat *materials, silk and laces, etc.. All of this had to be sewn before the wedding. Each towel, pillow case and sheet had to be initialed with embroidery. The whole thing was sent out to people that specialized in doing that work. Of course, it had to be finished by a certain date. Also my grandfather sent his wife and my mother to Kiev to [update] themselves with the latest fashions and buy every little matching accessory.*

Then of course there was the Jewish custom that the bride had to have her hair cut off so she would wear a wig for the rest of her married life. It is a terrible custom and has brought tears to many a young woman. Did you ever think the same custom held true in the Christian religion? The nuns or sisters also had to have their hair removed and thus always wore a hat gear. So it wasn't really so strange for a real orthodox family to do those things. My mother being somewhat of a liberal at heart put up a fierce fight. She was not going to have her hair cut. She didn't care if she never got married and if her family insisted, she was going to leave Russia and live with her brother in Rumania. Finally, after many a battle and many tears she won, and she got married with her own hair on her head.

At that time in Russia, the Jews who were well off had a beautiful and precious custom. Not only were the relatives from near and far, friends, business associates and the whole congregation invited to the wedding, and of course, friends, but all the poor of the town: the widows, widowers, the orphans and the sick, etc. The house was over-flowing with relatives who stayed for weeks before {and} after the wedding. The street was roped off [and] for the poor there [was] a table laden with food. The wedding reception extended into the well-kept beautiful garden. My grandfather went around and gave money to the poor, he gave money to each one from his own hands, he did not miss a soul. Of course, the poor enjoyed the live orchestra and danced those beautiful Jewish dances. The wedding lasted for days. My mother and father sat on two separate chairs and the men carried them in the chairs on their shoulders so everyone could greet them and cheer them on.

After this beautiful wedding my mother went to live at her in-laws' house. She didn't cook or help with the house work - she was a guest. She followed the rules and regulations of the orthodox religion to a tee. She was a good daughter-in-law.

The second year the young couple went to live with the [bride's] parents. My mother and father were also well-behaved. They obeyed the religious rules and my father liked to work with my grandfather. Things went smoothly, but behind the surface unbeknownst to my grandfather and grandmother things were happening, things were being done they never dreamed of.

As I said my mother, at heart, was a liberal. My grandfather had a habit that when he retired for the night the whole family had to retire at the same time. He went and locked each door and closed and locked the windows. His wife and their married children had to go to sleep at the same time. My mother and father also went to bed, as their elders did, but they waited till my grandfather and grandmother were asleep and snoring. Then my mother and father dressed and [along] with the other young folks in the house, they climbed through a window. They went to the barn and got on their horses, stopped [to meet up with] a couple [of] other friends and together they rode into the woods and had a night picnic. They sang and they danced, and joked and ate [to] their hearts content. At a certain time they all went home, climbed through the window, undressed again, and went to sleep. My grandparents never caught them, the servants were sworn to secrecy and they never squealed. They didn't do this too often, but they did do it. My father, being a very religious and obedient [man], didn't really at first approve of [this], but he loved my mother very much and thus went along with the deal. He was quiet but he was young and [in the] end admitted he enjoyed it also.

Then my mother liked to play cards, never for money, God forbid. She liked to play just for the fun of it and once in a while when my father and grandfather were away on business she and a couple of girlfriends locked themselves in a bedroom late at night, and they played cards.

After the year of living with my mother's parents was over, [my parents] bought themselves their home. They fixed it up the way they wanted it and moved into it. My mother had a young Jewish cook who lived in, as well as a housekeeper who also lived in [the house]. She had a Christian stable boy who also took care of the garden.

My mother had many relatives and friends [invited] in her new home. When my Uncle Yolick and his wife visited they would stay for a couple of days. My mother insisted they stay longer. When they refused, drastic action was taken. All of their shoes were hidden and thus they could not leave and missed their train which would not come again though the town till the following week. So after the train left they [were] given their shoes back, and everyone enjoyed each other's company. Might as well, the house rocked with laughter and merriment along with singing and dancing. They had a phonograph going till the wee hours. When the house was over-flowing with guests there was not enough beds. They did the next best thing. The men had one bedroom which had two large double size beds, and the women used the other bedroom of the same size. And, if need be, they slept along the width of the bed so each bed held four people instead of two. My father and mother were happy, and they loved each other and respected each other.

My mother was a beauty but frail. She seemed to always have stomach trouble. At times she traveled to Kiev to see a bigger, more well-

known doctor to see if he could help her. Those times that she stayed [in] Kiev she visited her relatives. Then, she found a rooming house and rented a room and went to this famous doctor. During that time she took advantage of her stay in Kiev and she shopped for yard goods to make the latest fashionable clothes. She bought perfume and shoes, etc. At night she did the unheard of thing, she went to the theater. Of course, her parents were never told that. In fact, besides being ill and being treated, she had a ball in the big city.

My mother had six children. One was still born, two died in an epidemic and three lived. The three who survived were my sister Anna (Hanula), my brother Jack and I, Ita, was the youngest. All of my older brothers and sisters were born at home. I was the only child born in a hospital. My mother never nursed her children. She hired a wet nurse for all of her babies except me who was her youngest.

My parents did manage to send my sister and brother to the Christian school. The fee was high and the bribe was steep, but to school they went. My brother had [a] head on his shoulders. He looked at his lesson but once and he remembered [it] all. He was good in school and never had to study at all. Thus, when my mother sent him to his room to study, he looked at the work once or twice and memorized [it]. [Then] he sneaked out the door and went to see what mischief he could get himself into.

My sister Hunala (Anna), on the other hand, took longer for her studies to sink in, but she was patient and willing to learn. She did much reading besides studying, and to find out what to read she wrote letters to prominent Russian authors. She told them her right age and asked for their suggestions and being that she was a child, not a competitor, they were flattered, and they sent her the best advice which she took advantage of. So not only did she do well at school at these given subjects she knew other information that the teacher in her class did not know about. Her teacher was not very happy to have a student like her. She always got the best marks. He had to give them to her [because] she earned it, [however] her marks were always eighty. She cried bitter tears that with all her answers correct on her tests she never got more than an eighty. After a long time, she got the courage together to ask her teacher why he was giving her eighty when her answers were all correct. His answer was, "Only God knew all the answers and it is He that gets the one hundred, the teacher gets ninety and the best student gets eighty." Then and only then did she stop crying over her school marks.

Ita Pogrebiski

My Mother's Wedding

In the Russian Pale of Settlement most Jews resided in *shtetls*. A *shtetl* is a *Yiddish* word which means small town. The number of inhabitants could be anywhere from 1,000, in which case it was called a *shtetle* (little *shtetl*), to 20,000. A shtetl was not technically a village, although that is how it is often described, because the law that created The Pale, did not allow Jews to live in villages. If a *shtetl* was upgraded to village status, the Jewish inhabitants were forced to move. This was depicted in the Broadway show *Fiddler on the Roof,* (1964) when Tevye and his family moved out of their shtetl, Anatevka, once it was deemed a village by the government. The *shtetl*, *mestechko* in Russian, was home to most of the Jews till the demise of The Pale in 1917.

My mother spent the first two years of her life in the shtetl Priluki which she said was near the city of Kiev. This information concurs with the shtetl listed as her place of origin in the manifest of the *SS Majestic*, the ship that brought her and her mother to the United States. Today, the town is in the Ukraine and it is spelled Pryluky. Her father's family lived in a shtetl called Zivitov or Zhivotovka. Because of the fluctuating political scene in that part of the world in the early part of the twentieth century, the names and spelling of the towns have changed.

There was a shtetl in The Pale named Pogrebishche. Based on the manner in which Jews took on surnames in the early 1800's, there is a good possibility that my mother's paternal ancestors came from this town.

Jews did not have surnames until the government under Tsar Alexander I issued an edict in 1804. The reasons listed in the edict were threefold, "Better establishment of the Citizenship conditions, for better protection of their property and for reviewing litigation between them." However, the regulation was not followed as intended; many Jews hated it and thus ignored the law. In 1835, Tsar Nicholas I issued a more rigorous law.

Before it was required, Jewish surnames only went back one generation. For instance, if Isaac had a son named Jacob, Jacob was known as Jacob *ben* Isaac; *ben* means son of. Women would have their father's first name for their surname, so a woman's name might be Leah bat Jacob; *bat* is daughter of. These names were used in religious services in the synagogue, on legal documents like the wedding *Ketubah* (wedding contract) or on headstones. That tradition continues to this day.

There was no set rule for the name one chose. There were trends and that depended on the area you lived. Around Kiev it was common to add *ski* to show it was a place name: town, shtetl, or city. My mother's surname, Pogrebiski, meant that her paternal ancestors got their name from a town where they may have once resided. Other adopted last names could describe one's livelihood; Isaac the goldsmith was now Isaac Goldsmith. Surnames could be a nickname, a family name, or could refer to appearance. Although some of the following are German surnames, the idea was the same: small (Klein), beautiful (Shone), dark complexion (Schwartz). Those who were the descendants of Moses' brother Aaron, the first of the ancient temple priests, took on the surname Kohane or Cohen.

***

The shtetl originated in Poland-Lithuania. As Jews were expelled from Austria, Hungary, and Germany, as well as from Spain and Portugal during the Inquisition, they were welcomed and offered sanctuary by King Zygmunt I, who reigned from 1506 to 1548. His son, Zygmunt II continued his father's magnanimity and granted the Jews jurisdiction over their own affairs including collecting their own taxes. The warm welcome and favorable conditions attracted refugees from all over Europe and the Mediterranean. Poland-Lithuania became simultaneously a haven and a heaven for the wanderers. The Jews entered into this symbiotic relationship by settling in remote areas and providing a needed service in bolstering the foreign trade of their adopted homeland. This was possible because of their international trading expertise and their advantageous connections in the countries where they originated. The Jewish economy thrived, and so did the foreign trade of Poland-Lithuania. This continued for 200 years until jealousy reared its ugly head in the form of a resentful middle class, supported by the church, who forced the government to restrict the Jewish trade. When the Jews lived peaceably without interference there was prosperity which, in turn, was fertile ground for trouble. This story would repeat itself; only the location would change.

With the annexation of Polish territory into the Russian regime, the shtetl in The Pale became the center for Jewish life, the foundation of which revolved around the synagogue, the home, and the market place. Like a three legged stool, each support was necessary to provide stability for the continuance of harmony and tradition.

The synagogue was integral to the religious life of the shtetl Jew. It was a house of prayer, the place where Jews connected with God and learned how to live according to God's laws. It was where one went to read and hear the Torah, *(Pentateuch)* the five books of Moses. Starting at the age of thirteen, men, with their heads covered and bodies wrapped in prayer shawls, were expected to pray three times a day. Synagogue attendance was not compulsory for women since the home was their sphere. If they attended, they were seated separately, with their heads covered and modestly dressed, behind a *mehitzah* or screen, so they would not be a distraction to the men.

The synagogue, simultaneously, served as a center of prayer and education. The Yiddish word for synagogue is *shul* which also means school. Young boys started their education shortly after they were weaned. They learned how to read Hebrew so they could read and understand the Torah. Older students and adult males discussed, argued, and debated the interpretation of the 613 commandments found in the Torah. This involved everything from what food was considered kosher to what activity was acceptable on the Sabbath, the day of rest. Education was so central to the lives of the Jews, that for the few families who could afford it, the men never worked. The spent their days in scholarly pursuit and prayer. The women handled the "store front."

The main reason for the enormous amount of time the men spent in study was simple. The commandments written in the Torah were not clear nor could they be carried out as written; clarification was needed to guide the community. Thus, the oral law, as the Talmud was first called, evolved. The commentary in the Talmud clarified what was ambiguous and offered an alternative. For instance, the biblical command, "an eye for an eye," cannot and should not be taken literally. It is often impossible to retaliate in that way. The Talmud offered a more rational and humane response in the way of monetary recompense for damages. Today, many governments follow Talmudic law when they have been wronged or have caused harm. An example of this is the reparations agreement between Germany and the State of Israel for the loss of lives and property during the Holocaust. Those lives could not be replaced nor would it be appropriate to kill six million German citizens in kind. A monetary payment from Germany has been the solution.

Most of the commandments did not offer enough instruction on how they were to be carried out. The following are two examples that make that point.

The fourth commandment is about resting on the seventh day and honoring the Sabbath. What exactly does that mean? What is the definition of resting and working? Work for one could be rest for another, so how do you differentiate? Can food be made on the Sabbath, since that is work, and if not, are you supposed to go hungry? Can medical personnel work on the Sabbath? Can you have a non-Jew do the work for you? When exactly should the holiday start and end? And, in this day of modern conveniences is driving a car considered working, or is walking, working?

This second example illustrates how one is considered Jewish. In ancient times one's Jewishness was patrilineal. But what happened when the Jews were conquered by gentiles and rape occurred? Who was the father then, and was the child, a result of rape, considered Jewish? Could you even be sure that the rapist was indeed the father? What about converts? What about adopted children?

The list of questions could go on and on, and it is with these issues that the scholars at the *yeshivas* (higher education where the Torah is studied) and *shuls* deliberated. They wrote their conclusions, regarding religious, legal and non-legal matters as commentary in the Talmud which provided the minutiae, or fine points. This allowed Jews, worldwide, to have the same guiding principles. The Talmud is never complete, but continually evolves as new questions arise due to changing conditions and modernization. For the Jews of the shtetl, the information found in the Torah and the Talmud, facilitated the rabbi to resolve disputes, decide thorny legal issues, and pass judgment on religious and secular impasses in the community.

The synagogue provided the social structure for the community. It was not only a meeting place, but one's status was always on display. The ark, which housed the sacred Torah scrolls, was located on the eastern side of the synagogue, the side that faced Jerusalem. This was the most coveted place to sit because of its close proximity to the Holy Scripture. These first class seats were reserved for the elite of the community: the rabbi's male relatives, professionals, prosperous businessmen, and great scholars. Likewise, the water carriers, the peddlers, and the poor sat the furthest from the ark. Knowing your place was as simple as finding your seat.

The traditional Jewish home in the shtetl was an extension of the synagogue. The home provided the opportunity where the family could live their religion by following the laws they learned from the Torah. It is where the Sabbath was happily ushered in every Friday at sundown with the woman of the home lighting candles and saying a blessing. This was followed with more blessings over the wine, the food and the children. Next, there was a festive meal which was prepared adhering to strict dietary laws. The evening culminated late in the night with loud boisterous singing. It was customary and considered a *mitzvah* (good deed) to invite guests including travelers, visiting *Yeshiva* students, and the needy to a welcome respite. Likewise, other holidays were celebrated with family and guests gathered around a table laden with traditional foods. A life cycle event, like a wedding, was often celebrated in and around the home and included the entire community. These events were not meant to be celebrated in isolation. It was a community affair which all had a stake in to maintain and ensure the continuance of tradition and acceptable behavior. Behavior "beyond the pale" was a guarantee of ostracism in one's personal and business life.

The market was a gathering place where the shtetl Jew socialized with other Jews, interacted with gentiles who they mistrusted, and briefly came in contact with the outside world. Besides purchasing locally made goods, there was an opportunity to obtain rarer merchandise from outside The Pale. Most Jews earned their living as shopkeepers, peddlers, water carriers, traders, artisans and middlemen; the majority was poor. The market place was an essential vehicle to eke out a living so one could afford a chicken in the pot for the Sabbath.

***

The shtetl's often drab exterior of ramshackle wooden structures and unpaved streets were misleading. Some writers have been unkind in their stereotypical descriptions of the shtetl, but what they failed to understand was, appearances were deceiving. There was a distinct colorful vibrancy that existed amongst its inhabitants in education, literature, theater, health and welfare, and life cycle events.

If the shtetl was large enough there was a community-funded *Yeshiva*. The top male students from all over The Pale would convene with the best teachers, to be educated with a recognized curriculum. Along with the *Yeshiva*, there were Jewish schools where Yiddish was spoken and Hebrew was taught. Parents preferred to keep their children in Jewish schools away from Christian influence and Russian indoctrination.

Yiddish was the primary language spoken in the shtetl all over Eastern Europe and The Pale. It was a combination of Hebrew and German with a smattering of several other languages. After the Holocaust, Yiddish was a language in trouble. Many who spoke the language died in the camps, and after World War II, young Jews, and especially

47

Israelis, preferred Hebrew which was expanded and modernized. In the United States, Jewish immigrants, and their children wanted to forget their past: the shtetl, the ghetto and the camps. They wanted to be modern Americans, so they stopped using Yiddish which they believed made them seem quaint, foreign and weak.

Yiddish was my mother's first language. While living in Europe it was the only one she spoke fluently although she did recognize a few Russian words. Shandel was fluent in Yiddish and Russian. Once they both came to the United States, my mother learned English as a second grader in public school, but Shandel spoke Yiddish until the day she died in 1950. I was born after Shandel passed away, and therefore, there was no need to speak Yiddish in my parent's home any more. The only time my mother and father spoke the language was when they didn't want me to know what was being said.

The reason for the decline in the number of Yiddish speakers was demonstrated in my family through death and immigration, and would be mirrored many times over in Jewish homes all over after World War II. Today there is a revival, of sorts. Luckily, there are still a few fluent old folks, and some newcomers who have taken on the task to bring back the language. Yiddish courses are now being offered at some American universities.

Many Yiddish words have become a part of our everyday vernacular. The following have a Yiddish origin: schlep (to carry), oy vey (oh, my), spiel (sales pitch), nosh (eat casually), chutzpah (guts), tush (a person's rear end), schmooze (talker), *kaput* (imminent fall) and bagel.

Literature flourished in the shtetl. The People of the Book also read newspapers available in four different languages: Russian, Yiddish, Hebrew and Polish. Various authors wrote about the shtetl experience and became well-known. Yiddish author Sholem Aleichem wrote *Tevye the Dairyman* in 1894 which was the basis for *Fiddler on the Roof*. Author, poet, playwright and activist S. Ansky wrote the internationally acclaimed drama *The Dybbuk,* and Mendele Mocher Storm wrote satirical pieces and was considered the "Grandfather of Yiddish Literature."

The theater was alive and well in the shtetl. Jews were playwrights, directors, and actors. There were traveling theater groups who found audiences all over The Pale and in Eastern Europe. All was performed in Yiddish. Plays were on any topic from the Bible to Shakespeare as well as depicting life in the shtetl.

The Jews of the shtetl took on the responsibility of the health and well-being of the members of their community in many different ways. First, all homes had a charity box displayed and each family donated what they could. The money collected was used to help those who were ill, brides with no dowry, orphans, the homeless, the widowed, and they supported brethren who lived in the Holy Land. Second, they built and maintained the *mikvah* (ritual bath) which was used regularly, but separately, by men and women. This cleanliness resulted in higher birth rates and an infant mortality rate that was half of the non-Jewish population. Bathing consistently also reduced the number of Jewish deaths whenever there was mass sickness of the general population. This also created problems. The afflicted thought the Jews had magical powers or were purposely spreading the sickness, but somehow weren't affected themselves. Ironically, many Jews were murdered because they were cleaner. Third, one of the first acts of any newly created Jewish community was to set aside land for a cemetery, and a *Chevra Kadishah,* (holy society) was organized.

The purpose of the Chevra Kadishah was to cleanse the deceased, wrap the remains in a shroud, and prepare it for internment while treating the body with the utmost respect. This preparation had to be done quickly since there was no embalming, and the body was buried within twenty-four hours. Female corpses were tended to by an all-female group, likewise for men. Membership in this group was most honored because it was one that few wish to join. There is a Chevrah Kadishah wherever Jews reside.

Weddings were an example of the dynamism of the shtetl. The arranged marriage was a public and lavish affair. The celebration lasted for days and included the entire family, from near and far, and the entire community, friend or not. There was no need for a formal invitation; the custom was for everyone to attend. Weddings were an opportunity for the families of the bride and groom to put their success and good fortune on display, and who wouldn't want to be a part of that. The inclusion of so many guests witnessing the wedding ensured the betrothal agreement between the two families. In addition, a *Ketubah* (wedding contract) written in Aramaic was signed by the groom and two male witnesses just prior to the ceremony. This legal document was not signed by the bride because it listed only the groom's obligations to her. It was meant to ensure the rights of the woman in a male dominated society and was read aloud at the ceremony. The *Ketubah* became the bride's property, her marriage insurance policy.

The wedding festivities were broken down into two parts. The first involved the young bride surrounded by her birth family and unmarried girlfriends. It was a sad and final opportunity to remember the past, bid farewell to her youth and innocence before entering the realm of married life. One custom that exemplified this transformation was the cutting of the bride's long hair. Her hair, considered an enhancement to her youth and beauty, her crowning glory, was no longer needed as she became a married woman. The new bride was

51

expected to keep her hair short or shave her head entirely, and cover her pate with a *babushka* (kerchief) or a wig for the rest of her life.

The second phase of the wedding began with the *bedeken*, the veiling of the bride. This tradition can be traced to a story in Genesis when the Patriarch Jacob was fooled by his future father-in-law, Laban, into marrying the wrong woman, Leah instead of Rachel. This happened because Laban wanted his oldest daughter married first. He had Leah heavily veiled and Jacob did not realize he had been conned until it was too late. At the *bedeken,* the groom makes sure he has the right woman before the veil is lowered. He does not see her again until the wedding ceremony.

The ceremony began when the groom was escorted by his family to the *chuppah*, the wedding canopy, followed by the veiled bride ushered in by her female relatives. Before all the wedding guests, the bride circled her groom seven times. There are many different interpretations for this tradition. One of those is when Joshua and his army marched around Jericho seven times, the walls came crumbling down. So should, metaphorically speaking, any barrier between the bride and groom. Then, under the *chuppah,* surrounded by the couple's immediate family, the ceremony led by a rabbi, included seven blessings, sharing a cup of wine, the groom placing an unadorned solid gold band on the bride's index finger, and ending with the groom stomping on a wine glass.

There are many interpretations for breaking the glass. My mother told me was it was a reminder that even in our greatest moment of joy, we remember, with sorrow, the destruction of the Temple in Jerusalem. Another explanation is that since it would be impossible to return the glass to its original condition, so too, the bride and groom could never go back to who they were prior to the wedding. Now with the seriousness of the ceremony over, there was only joy.

There were many elements to create the perfect wedding. Mandatory, was the *klezmer* (type of music) band which played throughout the many days of the wedding culminating in lively tunes so all could dance. Klezmer bands got their start in Eastern Europe. They consisted of four to five male musicians usually led by a first violinist. The type of instruments played varied by region. The two families demonstrated their happiness and unity by dancing together, although men and women did this separately. The bride and groom were carried high on chairs surrounded by and cheered on by their dancing guests.

Leading the wedding festivities was a paid master of ceremonies or entertainer, a *badkhn*. His role was to bring laughter to the young couple by telling jokes, reciting comical rhymes, singing parodies, or just clowning around. His role was to do whatever was necessary to satisfy the religious commandment of bringing joy to the bride and groom.

***

The vibrancy of shtetl life was at its height during the golden age of The Pale from 1790 to 1840. For five decades Jews in the shtetl were rarely harassed, their lives were stable, and along with economic opportunity they flourished. After 1840, life became increasingly difficult. The decline was due to Russian nationalism and militarization. Furthermore, xenophobic Russians were blinded by their bigotry and jealousy, which created untenable living conditions for the Jews. In other words, the Russians tried to make the Jews of The Pale more Russian by attempting to purge their culture. With that, the end was in sight.

The final curtain fell on The Pale in 1917 when it was delegitimized. The shtetls within the former Pale sputtered along on their downward spiral due to the mass exodus of Jews for safer shores. It was then totally wiped out with the Nazi invasion as millions of the remaining shtetl inhabitants were either killed in mass shootings by the *Einsatzgruppen* (Nazi death squads) or marched off to the death camps.

Sherry V. Ostroff

This *ketubah* is for the wedding of my parents, Ita Pogrebiski and Herman Vernick. The date is Saturday, August 17, 1940. The Hebrew date is the 7th day of the week, 13th day of *Av*, 5700. The minister, Emanuel Barkan, was a cousin and a cantor, (religious singer). The witness, Nathan Grubman, was a first cousin. The other witness is unknown. The foreign text is Aramaic. Both of my parents signed the ketubah, but in The Pale only the groom would have signed.

55

Left to right: Shandel Rabbin Pogrebiski, age 34; Ita Pogrebiski, age 3, Jack Pogrebiski, age 15. Ages are approximate. Picture taken in Balti, Rumania. The year is about 1921.

Conditions in Russia
The Pogrom

Tsar Nicholas [II] did not want the Russian masses to be educated especially the peasants, the farmers and the Jews. He wanted the peasants to be unlearned and ignorant. He needed them to grow the crops, serve in his army and not complain. Thus, there were few schools throughout Russia. Only the Jewish people put up a fight and tried to send their children to school. At best, only a certain percent [of the Jews], who could afford it, went to the Russian schools. The rest were content studying the Bible, the Talmud and the Gemara. The poor poverty-ridden Jews had little time to study, but all studied to some degree. The heads of the synagogue took the poverty-stricken children and the orphans and taught them to pray free of charge.

Taxes were high, but the Jew had to pay even higher taxes than all the others.

Transportation was poor and a problem. Most people traveled by horses, horse and wagon, [or] coach and horses. Trains were few and only traveled to main cities. To get to a train you had to first get to the railroad station by horse. The trains were infrequent and laid over for hours before they continued on their route.

The people had to get visas and special permission to travel from one place to another in their own country. You were permitted to travel by the date stated on the card. If you were delayed and the date expired, you were fined and had to pay to start all over again with a new card and new permits. Every family was searched and papers recorded how many children were in the family, the ages of the sons and when they would be of age to go into the armed forces. Bribery only helped for a few months, then they would [come] back and force the young men into the service. If you objected you were sent to Siberia. If you spoke up and complained you were sent to Siberia, and never knew if you would return, [or if] you would be killed there or would die from the bitter cold.

The Russians were a mighty people and had a mighty army. They were always fighting some country and most of the time they lost because they drank too much and got drunk. Of course, the Jew suffered most of all. He served and served no matter who won. He was forced to serve many more years than the Christian Russians. When and if the Jewish soldier ever came back they were broken up bodily and mentally. They lost track of time and relatives.

When the Christian holidays came around, such as Christmas or Easter, the people and the church went on a rampage. The masses drank and got themselves in such a state that they wanted to get even with the Christ killers. They would tear through the town and break store windows, beat up Jews in the streets and break into some homes. All the Jews, during these holidays, closed their stores, hid themselves in their homes, bolted the windows and doors, and all of this happened during the peaceful times.

Then there was a change. The up and coming Communists made pogroms. They traveled in bands from one town to another, from one village to another and they killed all the people they could find. They killed the rich, the middle class and the Jews. The king's armed forces reacted to the pogroms by killing the poor, the workers and the Jews. Village after village, town after town were set on fire. They killed men, women and children. The women they raped, and then killed them.

The peasants around where my mother lived came running into town telling the Jewish people that a band of murderers were approaching, and they were mostly killing the Jews. They had a meeting with the Jewish men and told them that the Jews in this community had nothing to fear. They, the Christians, had been living peacefully with the Jews. They had been selling their crops to the Jews and for years they made a living, and they were not going to let them down. [The Christians] were now not going to let the bands through unless they were going to kill them first. These Christian kept their promise and the bands changed their direction, and not one Jew was hurt.

Then it happened again. Other bands were heading to town. Every town they passed thus far,

*they killed and raped and robbed and burned
houses down. But, the same group of Christians,
the very same ones that saved the Jews before, told
the Jews that again they would help them and save
them from destruction. It was their duty to do this
being that [they] were such good neighbors. Who
else would [they] sell [their] crops to? They
advised that the women and children to stay at their
homes and the men should gather at the wall of the
sugar factory. The Jewish men should show up in
strength, every man and youth should be there.
Since the peasants knew all the Jews in town they
saw which ones were missing and they sent some
men to go find them so all could be together. A few
men were not found, for instance, a few hid in the
high over-grown corn fields. My uncle, [my
mother's brother-in-law] hid in an outhouse. He let
himself down into the mire. The rest of the Jews
stood at the sugar factory wall and the Christians
stood in front and were ready to deal with the
"pogromishchakis". The bands came with fast
running horses and swords to the group of
Christians and Jews. The Christians group parted
and let the bands rush in on the unarmed Jews
standing against the wall and the band decapitated
each and every Jew and my father was one of them.*

*The bands stormed through the towns. They
raped and murdered women and children, robbed
and burned houses down. When my mother heard
the screaming and crying she knew what was
happening. She gathered her children and hid in a
cellar deep under the ground. The house above*

them was burned down, as were many others, and also the home of her father. The maid of her mother refused to hide. She said this band was for the working class and since she was a maid, she was safe, but when the band started breaking up and stealing, she started to scream, so they killed her also.

On the day my mother became a widow she had three children to care for. Her house was burned to the ground and an old father and mother to care for. All the money was gone. All that there was, [was] gone

Then came a time [when] the bands came one after another. My grandparents died from starvation. Between bands my brother and sister roamed the streets to see if they could find some food. I existed only on water and a little sugar. My mother said I seemed to sense that there was something wrong and I never cried out.

When more bands were coming through, the Jews that were left planned where they would hide: dark unknown passages, attics, and cellars. Those people who had children had a hard time getting a hiding place as the children might cry out or whimper and thus reveal the hiding place and everybody would get killed.

Once, my mother, who was carrying me, ran in the dark to hide. I hit my head [on] a wall but I didn't give a whimper. Everybody was hungry.

They were starving and hiding, day and night, like rats. The other Jews helped my mother to see that there was a little sugared water for me.

Then between the in-coming bands, my mother decided to somehow escape. She heard rumors that somehow some people did manage to escape, so with the help and plans of some people that were willing to chance [it] she managed to escape with her children to the town of Zivitov [Zivotovka] where my father's parents lived. My grandfather had died and there was only my grandmother and her daughter living. My grandmother grieved, of course, [over] my father's death [but] she was not so willing or happy to take my mother and [her] children in, but, will or not, we stayed in her house. There had been some pogroms in this town also. They were robbed a number of times, but as the saying goes, my grandmother had the luck and the knack to hide certain things in certain places. She hid money and jewelry and silverware. The bands and the peasants found all the stuff hidden by other members of the family but never did they find what my grandmother hid. She had the knack to hide it in the most obvious places and there it stayed hidden.

Because my mother was made to feel miserable [since] she was not contributing to the support of herself and the children, she decided to travel to a certain town where some people owed my father some money from a previous business deal. She left my sister and brother and me in my [grandmother's] care and went to that town. My grandmother didn't really take very good care of me. I was greatly neglected, so I was told. Well anyway, one way or another, I fell down and hit my head against an iron bar and fractured my skull. I do not remember any of this happening. My mother told me this in later years. I was taken every day to a doctor, that is my brother carried me to him daily. I was heavy and crying and the doctor's house was quite a distance away. But, he carried me, nonetheless. If it hadn't been for my brother and the doctor, I would have died.

One time, so my brother related, he got me to the doctor and when he took off my clothes and the diaper, my brother saw that I [soiled] it. [My brother] was young and sensitive and he was so ashamed that for many years he kept telling me about this humiliating experience.

My mother arrived at the house where these people owed us money. She was welcomed, well rested and fed. They gave her the money they owed her. She tied it around her waist under her underwear. She was ready to leave the family when all of a sudden they heard screaming and yelling and crying. Someone hollered in Yiddish, "Hide for your lives." The lights were blown out immediately and they started to crawl on their hands and knees to some hiding place in a deep underground cellar under the house. There they stayed hidden. One of them would venture out a little distance to hear if it had quieted down. Finally, they heard someone

*holler in Yiddish that all was clear. They came of
their hiding place and my mother started to ask
around if somehow she could get a horse and thus
leave town.*

*Many Jews tried to get out of the town.
They had a feeling that trouble was just beginning.
My mother heard that a wagon [full] of people was
going to leave that night. So she managed to get
herself on it.*

*The children were placed inside the wagon.
The men and women were seated around the edge
of the wagon with their feet dangling out so to make
more space for more people. So in the dead of night
they started out to go to the next town where they
heard there was no trouble yet. Things were quiet
yet. So, on they traveled through the dark of night
in deep grief and silence, mile after mile in the
middle of nowhere. As they were traveling,
suddenly a band of soldiers appeared with guns and
surrounded the wagon and made everyone
disembark. They beat everyone with the butts of the
guns. They didn't shoot because it seemed they
didn't want the shots heard. They made everyone
undress, men, women and children. They robbed
every one of the jewelry and money they could find
and of course they stole the money my mother was
carrying. They beat everyone: men, women and
children. They beat my mother, she begged them to
stop. Between beatings she kissed their shoes [to
get them] to stop, and she realized that they had no
intention to stop, so she dropped to the ground and*

64

*she decided to play dead. That's what saved her.
They went around from body to body and kicked
everyone to make sure they were dead, and they
kicked my mother. She played dead and they finally
left. When all was still, my mother thought she was
the only one alive. In the dark she crawled from
body to body [and she] tried to see if someone was
alive. Finally, she did find someone alive, a man.
She and he were the only ones that had survived.
They dressed in some of the clothes that were lying
around. The horses were gone, so they did the only
thing that was left to do, start walking. They
decided to separate and walk in different directions
because if again a band [came upon them] they
would surely kill them both, but going in separate
directions, maybe at least one of them would get to
safety. Thus my mother stumbled and walked and
fell and got up and forced herself to keep moving.
She was bleeding from head to toe, she was black
and blue all over and her eyes were so swollen she
could hardly see. Every tree from a distance looked
like a man with a gun, but she kept on [going]. As
she approached the supposed man with a gun, she
consoled herself it was just another tree. Toward
early dawn she came upon another wagon full of
women peasants going to the fields to work. They
stopped and asked what happened [because] she
was so bloodied up and so beaten up. My mother
told them the truth and the women shook their
heads and showed their pity. They wanted to clean
her up, clean the blood off, but they had no water.
So, they urinated and with a rag they washed off the
blood. They showed my mother which direction she*

should take to the nearest town. They told her there were Jews in that town and they advised her if she met anyone [on] the road she should not tell what happened to her. She should tell them she fell off a horse. Thus my mother finally reached the edge of the town and at the sight of the first person she fainted away.

When she woke she found herself in a bed bandaged up, in great pain and in a Jewish home. There she stayed for weeks till finally she was able to go to where my grandmother lived.

When my mother got to my grandmother's house, [we were barely existing]. Then the bands started to come to my grandmother's town to kill, rob and rape.

I don't know what happened to my grandmother and her daughter, but I do know of another episode that happened. The bands were coming again and again. Everyone was seeking a hiding place. Some Christians helped the bands and told them where the Jews were hiding and some did the opposite. This Christian couple who were childless and they wanted a child, so they struck up a bargain with my mother. Since I looked like a little Christian child with my blond hair and as yet unable to speak, they were willing to pretend I was their child. They would put a cross on me and kept me with them in their house. My mother, brother and sister would hide in their huge barn that was filled with hay. They would stay hidden in the hay

66

*and [the farmer] would throw in bread and water to
keep them alive. But, if in case the bands burned
down the barn and my family perished, I was to
become the Christian [couple's] daughter. So
that's what happened. [My family] stayed hidden in
the hay and when the bands came to search the
house [and] they were told I was their only child.*

*When bands came they didn't want to do
harm to the Christian family so instead of burning
down the barn they threw their swords at the hay.
When they couldn't see or hear anything they left.
But still it still wasn't safe for my mother and the
kids to come out for the pogroms were still going
on. The farmer would walk around the barn, make
believe he was looking around the barn and talking
as though to himself, and thus he informed my
mother what was going on and whose house was
still burning and who had been killed. After about a
week of destruction the band left. I was returned to
my mother and we were all saved. I do not
remember one incident of what happened. All this
was told to me by my mother.*

*The only thing I remember of this time is
when I was sitting on a step outside along with two
little boys. They were no bigger than me. (This was
in Vinnitsa). I didn't know who these boys were,
but it so happened they were my cousins and they
were a little older than I. My mother and I were
staying at my mother's sister's house. In fact, this
was when all was lost and my sister and brother
somehow had escaped to Romania and my mother*

and I were the only ones left in Russia. My Aunt Eta's husband was alive and well (remember he had hid in the outhouse). They lived in this little town that escaped the pogroms with his little family.

I didn't know it at the time but actually my mother was waiting for the time when she could escape from Russia and join my sister and brother. How they escaped from Russia I do not know. I never asked. In fact, I was so young I didn't even know I had a brother and sister.

Well anyway, my first memory of my life was sitting on the step with my cousins. We must have been told to sit very quietly as none [of us] made a sound. We must have been told not to move away since none of us attempted to do so. From the house you could hear singing. It was Maria, the maid, who was forever washing laundry. She was singing her Russian songs. [In] later years my mother taught me one of her songs. It was a very common song of the Russian peasant about the drinking problem. [It was about] this woman telling her husband that he should stop beating her. She was going to leave him with the children and go on a boat and go far, far away from home. She did just that. She goes on a boat and left. Then the song goes on where the husband finds her and he begs her to return home. He promises not to beat her and promises to live peacefully with her. He tells her the children need her and cry for her. She should return home. (This is a translation.)

68

I only remember snatches of being in Russia. In fact, I didn't even know about countries then. I remember sleeping on a sofa and falling. At other times I remember a woman, (which was my Aunt Eta), standing over a lot of candles and crying. Her hands [were] over her face. It must have been Friday evening and she was saying the [Sabbath] blessing and praying and crying at the same time.

Ita Pogrebiski

Conditions in Russia
The Pogroms

My mother was born in the wrong place at the wrong time. She came into this world in the midst of two Russian revolutions that spanned from 1917 to 1921. The first, the Revolution of 1917, was the forced abdication of the last Romanov ruler, Tsar Nicholas II. The ensuing civil war with the Bolsheviks and the defeat of the government forces was the second revolution. It was a time of great upheaval, rebellion, pogroms (anti-Jewish riots), mass murder and widespread destruction. The area formerly known as The Pale of Settlement became a dangerous place for a Jewish child in 1918.

The reasons for the tsar's abdication were many, but from the start, even at Nicholas' coronation in 1896, his reign began deplorably with the *Khodynka* Tragedy. The promise of bread, a piece of sausage, a commemorative cup and a gold coin brought almost half a million Russians to Moscow to cheer for their new ruler. There was not enough to go around and 1400 Russians were suffocated or crushed to death in a stampede. Although the newly crowned tsar and his tsarina Alexandra were unaware, at first, of the tragic event, once learning of the circumstances they continued on with the festivities unabated. This disregard for Russian lives did not bode well with the masses. They considered their tsar a father-figure. Tsar Nicholas was not acting like a benevolent parent. Not an auspicious start for a new ruler.

Nicholas was a man who should never have become tsar. Like most rulers throughout history it was an accident of birth which brought him to the throne. He stated to a close friend, "I am not prepared to be a tsar. I never wanted to become one. I know nothing of the business of ruling." Besides being ill-prepared, Nicholas believed that his right to rule was absolute, answerable only to God. An incompetent, ill-equipped autocrat, devoid of any natural leadership abilities, was a dangerous combination.

Throughout his reign, Nicholas and the Russian people experienced one calamity after another. It didn't help matters that Nicholas had inherited a mess from his father, Alexander III in 1894. During his father's reign almost half a million Russians starved in a famine that gripped the country. To redirect the anger of the starving peasants, Alexander endorsed their participation in pogrom after pogrom against the Jews.

When Nicholas assumed power he was beset with additional problems. From 1904 to 1905 Japan and Russia fought over perceived Russian aggression. The Japanese resented the Russian expansion of the Trans-Siberian Railroad to the Pacific coast. The war ended with the Russian fleet in ruins. Then, in 1905, hundreds of peaceful workers, led by Father George Gabon, demonstrated for better working conditions and the creation of a popular assembly. More than a thousand were shot and killed by government troops in front of the Winter Palace in St. Petersburg. The people blamed Nicholas, so the peasantry who supported the demonstrating workers went on strike. There were uprisings all over the country, and again, pogroms were endorsed as a diversion. The massacre in St. Petersburg came to be known as "Bloody Sunday." Consequently, the three tragedies that occurred on Nicholas's watch, Khodynka, the Kishinev pogrom in 1903, and Bloody Sunday, earned him the nickname "Bloody." Eventually, he had to concede and allowed for an elected assembly called the Duma. This was the Russian Revolution of 1905, the first of three in the first quarter of the twentieth century.

World War I was not going well for the Russians. Nicholas foolishly decided to dismiss his top general and take over military leadership. The army was still unsuccessful and more than 75% of the fighting force ended up dead or wounded. Russia had the highest casualty rate of any participating country, and Nicholas was held accountable. In addition, Nicholas' military responsibilities kept him away from his family and his son Alexei who suffered from hemophilia. Alexandra, desperate for a cure, engaged the highly suspect services of Gregori Rasputin, a peasant from Siberia. Completely under his spell, with his promise of restoring Alexei to good health, Alexandra, along with the semi-illiterate Rasputin, governed in her husband's absence. As a result, many of the cabinet ministers resigned, and chaos ensued. It didn't help that Alexandra was a German by birth, so her intentions were questionable especially during World War I. Some suspected she was purposely undermining the Russian government. All of these events led to the arrest and incarceration of the royal family. After twenty-three years on the throne, Nicholas, Alexandra, their four teenaged daughters, Olga, Marie, Tatiana and Anastasia, and their son, were executed on July 17, 1918 in Yekaterinburg.

***

Pogroms increased in number and severity whenever there were tumultuous events in modern Russian history: Tsar Alexander II's assassination in 1881; the Kishinev Pogrom in 1903; Bloody Sunday in 1905; the revolution and civil war from 1917-1921. The reasons for the difficult times had nothing to do with the Russian Jews; they were just a convenient scapegoat. The pogroms were government endorsed and supported by the church, the press and the military. It was of no consequence if the vigilantes were the peasants, the government forces (White Army), the Bolsheviks (Red Army) or the Ukrainians. The result was the same. It was during the last of these unsettling times, from 1917 to 1921, when the pogroms reached a new savagery. My mother and her family were among the unfortunate victims.

My mother stated that she and her family lived in the town of Priluki at the time a pogrom arrived. The date was July 4, 1919. She was one year old, so she was not told about the horror until she was old enough to understand. The pogrom bands were under the leadership of Ataman (headman) Sokolovski. At least sixteen towns were pillaged by him and his gang. In the end, they were responsible for killing 2,000 people. It is probable that after the violence subsided, my mother and her family escaped to another shtetl. They did not find shelter there because the snarling teeth of the pogrom bit down hard on them again one month later.

Most likely my mother and her family fled to Pogrebishche from Priluki. There are several reasons for this conclusion. First, as stated before, the paternal side of the Pogrebiski family probably came from Pogrebishche because they took the town's name as their own when Jews were forced to have surnames. Therefore, they may have had some familiarity with the town. Fleeing to a town where one had relatives, who could offer refuge, would seem an obvious destination under duress. Second, my mother described the attacks as happening multiple times. Pogrebische was attacked three times, Priluki once. Third, she claimed her father was killed at the wall of a sugar factory, and there was such a building at that time in Pogrebische. Fourth, and most startling, my mother's description of the events that led to her father's death is eerily similar to an eye-witness account.

This is the chain of events leading up to the pogrom in Pogrebishche given in a deposition by an eyewitness. On August 13th, a representative of Ataman Symon Petlura's met with the leaders of the Jewish defense unit. The meeting was cordial. The next day, the Jews were told their weapons were not necessary because they had nothing to fear. Petlura offered his guarantee of protection. On August 17, there was word that Ataman Anton Zeleny's band was coming. The Jewish men wanted to get their wives and children out of harm's way and retrieve the weapons they had hidden. Again, they were reassured by Petlura that no pogrom would occur under his watch. To make sure no one escaped he placed sentries at all the exits. On August 18, Zeleny's troops arrived, a massacre ensued and 400 were killed.

My mother related similar details. She did not mention the names of the atamans involved nor did she know the dates, but these facts are corroborated by a deposition given by B. O. Lifschitz. She said that the Jewish men were not allowed to leave the town. Her uncle went into hiding because he didn't trust those who said they would protect the Jews. A group went looking for him. The Jewish men were told not to fear the pogroms. Their safety was guaranteed. Just the opposite occurred. The Jewish men were deceived and trapped, including her father, and they were slaughtered by the sugar factory.

Zeleny and his gang, along with Petlura, have been blamed for the devastation at Progrebishche. Zeleny claimed that he was not in the shtetl at the time nor was he guilty in carrying out the atrocities, however, eyewitness accounts place him at the scene of the crime and those under his command carried out the pogrom. The leader of the Jewish community in Pogrebishche stated the following about Zeleny's forces. "They conducted a pogrom with all of the details. They robbed, raped and killed. They did not only want our possessions, but our souls as well. They removed people from cellars and attics and killed them...Neither old nor young were spared."

Zeleny was the son of a peasant and lived in a village near Kiev. His chaotic military career began as a member of the Bolshevik Army. Then, he dropped out of the army, claimed neutrality, and then fought against the Bolsheviks. Zeleny became the self-appointed charismatic leader of the peasantry and won them over with his oratory skills and filling their stomachs with food including the promise of white bread, a rare delicacy for the poor. Zeleny's goal, to capture Kiev, was something he never achieved, but Pogrebishche and many other shtetls were tragically in his path. To the Jews he was a murderer; to the peasants he was a folk hero.

What did Zeleny have against the Jews? He claimed in a speech that he was "...neither a Jew-lover nor a Jew-hater...but the land belongs only to the Ukrainians. The Jews cannot take offence at

77

this. The Jew does not need land." He believed the Jews had too much power, and it was right that the Ukrainians take that power away. At the same time, he believed it was right that the Jews should pay for the revolution to free Ukraine because they would reap some of the benefits once it was over. He added, "We must annihilate the cities of the Ukraine because they are strange to us and hateful toward us." This was code for the pogroms to commence. Shortly after the massacre at Pogrebishche, Petlura and Zeleny, were killed. Zeleny died in battle against the White Army near his home town in September, 1919. Petlura was assassinated in Paris in 1926 by former shtetl Jew Shalom Schwarzbard. Schwarzbard's family was murdered in a pogrom and he blamed Petlura. Schwarzbard was tried and acquitted in a French court. He died in 1938 and was interred in Israel in 1967.

***

Once the Jews in the shtetl realized the government was not going to protect them from pogroms, and in fact, were often the instigators of the violence, they created their own self-defense forces. This is contrary to the popular notion that the shtetl Jews were meek, cowardly, and did nothing to protect themselves or their families.

Where did this stereotype of the submissive and timid Jew come from? Oddly enough, it may be attributed to a Jew. An epic poem written by Hayyim Nahman Bialik was published in 1904, a

year after the Kishinev pogrom. The poem was
called *The City of Slaughter*. Bialik wrote that the
Jews bear some guilt for not fighting back, although
eyewitnesses claimed the opposite. A small portion
of the poem is below.

Descend then, to the cellars of the town,
There where the virginal daughters of thy folk were
fouled,
Where seven heathen flung a woman down,
The daughter in the presence of her mother,
The mother in the presence of her daughter,
Before slaughter, during slaughter, and after
slaughter!
Touch with thy hand the cushion stained; touch
The pillow incarnadined:
This is the place the wild ones of the wood, the
beasts of the field
With bloody axes in their paws compelled thy
daughters yield:
Beasted and swined!
Note also, do not fail to note,
In that dark corner, and behind that cask
Crouched husbands, bridegrooms, brothers, peering
from the cracks,
Watching the sacred bodies struggling underneath
The bestial breath,
Stifled in filth, and swallowing their blood!
Watching from the darkness and its mesh
The lecherous rabble portioning for booty
Their kindred and their flesh!
Crushed in their shame, they saw it all;
They did not stir nor move;

79

They did not pluck their eyes out; they
Beat not their brains against the wall!
Perhaps, perhaps each watcher had it in his heart to
pray:
A miracle, O Lord ¡ª and spare my skin this day!

An article on the front page of the April 24th, 1903
edition of the Yiddish newspaper *The Forward*
came to an opposite conclusion. "…Kishinev Jews
are tough, healthy, strong as iron and fearless.
When the murderous pogromists began their
horrible slaughter, Jewish boys and men came
running and fought like lions to protect their weaker
and older brothers and sisters. Even young girls
exhibited amazing heroism. They defended their
honor with supernatural strength…."

During each wave of pogroms, 1881-1882, 1903-
1905, and 1917-1921 the Jews fought back. In the
first wave, defense forces were established and
young men enlisted. Their weapons were sticks,
axes, and iron poles. Few had firearms. For
communication they used the sounds made from the
shofar, a ram's horn traditionally used to usher in
the Jewish New Year at Rosh Hashanah. Some in
the shtetl opposed such action thinking it would
further increase Russian hatred.

Defense units were created in 1903 to help protect
the 60,000 Jews who lived in Kishinev, located in
the province of Bessarabia. They suffered a two
day pogrom in which forty-nine were murdered,
hundreds wounded, and homes and businesses were

destroyed. The violence started due to the scurrilous age-old blood libel tale that lingered from the middle ages to the modern era among the illiterate superstitious folk. The blood libel accusation usually occurred with the confluence of two events. First, a gentile, usually a child, went missing or was found dead with no known perpetrator to blame. Second, it was the season of two major holidays, Easter and Passover. In the case in Kishinev, it was believed that the Jews killed a Christian so that the blood could be added to the making of matzah, the unleavened bread eaten during the eight days of Passover. It was of no importance to the attackers that the accusations made no sense. Jews are forbidden from consuming blood, but the blood-thirsty vigilantes needed a scapegoat to assuage their rage.

The town was already a powder keg due to the heightened tensions between the Christians and Jews. The local newspaper and the government were complicit by fanning the incendiary sparks into flames, and when violence broke out the military did not intervene. It did not help matters that Easter was always considered a dangerous time for Jews. My mother told me that when she still lived in Eastern Europe as a young girl, she had to stay indoors during Easter. It was too dangerous to be out on the streets if you were a Jew.

Kishinev, the first site of a major pogrom in the twentieth century, resulted in worldwide condemnation and mass demonstrations in major cities: New York, London and Paris. The young Jews of the shtetls reacted by creating defense units with proper training. Money was raised to purchase guns and blacksmiths made iron poles with spikes. Communication was now the telephone, the few that existed, and a network of spies was planted among the pogromists. Some young people sought a political solution and joined revolutionary groups whose focus was to overthrow the tsar. Thus, the march began towards revolution. Others, such as future Israeli Prime Minister David Ben-Gurion, left Russia and made their way to Palestine. Their experience in Russia and their belief in socialism led to the creation of the Kibbutz, the labor unions, and the self-defense forces. This would become the foundation of a future nation. Ironically, the pogroms created a sense of pride and Jewish nationalism for a people who had no country.

The pogroms of 1917-21 were different and so was the defense. The attackers were now largely professional soldiers which made resistance more difficult. On the other hand, as the government military was collapsing and Jewish soldiers returned home, they offered their experience and took on leadership roles in their local defense. The protection provided by defense units was at times successful until the experienced soldier-leader fell in battle. With the loss of the defense unit, the Jews were no match for the swarm that was coming.

***

The international Jewish response to the pogroms was a reawakening of political Zionism. Along with other events such as the Dreyfus Affair in France in 1894 and centuries of living in the diaspora, Jews realized they would never be secure without a homeland which more than ever had become a necessity. The Jewish community found an ally in British Prime Minister Lloyd George and Scottish Statesman Arthur Balfour. In 1917, Balfour proposed his Declaration, which was a letter indicating the British government's favor towards a homeland in Palestine for stateless Jews worldwide.

This proposal came about due to the convergence of two critical needs. The British, during World War I, required acetone for the war effort. Russian born, but now British citizen, Chaim Weizmann, was the leader of the Zionist movement and a biochemist. He invented a fermentation process to produce the acetone. The British needed the acetone, Weizmann wanted a Jewish homeland. It was a q*uid pro quo*. Unfortunately, the Balfour Declaration was not legally binding, and in 1939, the British government reneged. With the vicious Russian pogroms fading into memory and the world focused on the march of the Third Reich across Europe, the stage was now set for the worst pogrom of all, the Holocaust.

Sherry V. Ostroff

The wooden synagogue in Pogrebishche built in the 17th century.

Balfour Declaration

Foreign Office
November 2nd, 1917

Dear Lord Rothschild,

I have much pleasure in conveying to you, on behalf of His Majesty's Government, the following declaration of sympathy with Jewish Zionist aspirations which has been submitted to, and approved by, the Cabinet.

"His Majesty's Government view with favour the establishment in Palestine of a national home for the Jewish people, and will use their best endeavours to facilitate the achievement of this object, it being clearly understood that nothing shall be done which may prejudice the civil and religious rights of existing non-Jewish communities in Palestine, or the rights and political status enjoyed by Jews in any other country."

I should be grateful if you would bring this declaration to the knowledge of the Zionist Federation.

Yours sincerely,
Arthur James Balfour

The Escape

One night I found myself being carried on the shoulders of a man, (He was my Uncle Mendel) into the dark woods. My mother was walking at his side. I didn't cry out because my mother was there and I had no fear. They kept walking fast and never said a word to each other. They walked a long, long time, but I didn't care. I liked being carried on his shoulders. Then, I don't know how, but in the middle of woods we came upon a lone house. We went into that dark house and the room was very huge. On the floor was a little dim light. There was not a single piece of furniture in it. And all around against the wall sat men and women. Not a word was spoken. I don't know how long we stayed, but the next thing I knew we were outside again, my mother, my uncle and I, and this time all the people from the house joined us.

Once again, we all started walking briskly through the dark woods. Sometimes I was carried by my mother and some by my uncle, but most of the time I was made to run. But then a strange thing was happening in the middle of our walking everybody dropped to the ground, and what's more, my mother made me drop down too. I didn't know why she made me drop down and then made me walk and repeat the process over and over again. I could hear something fly by over our heads and make a whizzing sound. I [didn't] realize it was bullets that we were dodging.

The next thing I remember was when I woke up one morning and found myself in a single size bed sleep[ing] alongside a soldier fully dressed and with many buttons on his jacket. I got scared of him and more so of those buttons. Not seeing my mother about I started cry[ing] and scream[ing] for my mother. The soldier tried to quiet me, and in that room there were many more soldiers. They thought it was very funny and laughed. The soldier that I had been sleeping with took me by the hand (I was afraid when he tried to carry me) and he led me outside. There by a fence was my mother sitting on the ground with a shawl around her. She opened up her shawl and spread her arms around me and I was in sheer heaven, the protective arms of my mother. Then, I noticed that there were a lot of people sitting on the ground also against this fence. That's all I remember.

My mother told me later that there were two groups of people trying to escape Russia. The two groups walked in the dark of night in the deep woods and through cornfields. They traveled at night only till they came to this certain area. There they met an officer and he spoke to each group separately telling them that one group would be able to escape from Russia. We had to cross a river and the small rowboat could only hold one group. He [would] decide which group could go later, meanwhile, we would stay in hiding. The captain

88

*seemed to like my mother. He had a little talk with
her, gave me candy and petted me.*

    *The people were lowered into a deep cave.
It must have been huge and had a lot of over-growth
on top. Water and bread was lowered to them and
thus they stayed hidden for days. The people didn't
know if it was night or day. At times they thought
they were forgotten and the cave was a death trap.
Then at long last, one night, all the people were
lifted out of the cave.*

    *The people, again, were divided into two
groups as they had been before. In the center stood
a man all dressed in a long black cape and a hood
over his head covering his face. Only his eyes
showed through. He raised his arm one way and
directed one group to go there, and then directed
the other group to go in another direction. My
mother knew her group was crossing over as he sort
of winked at her on purpose so she wouldn't worry.*

    *I remember it being very dark standing with
my mother in a group of people at the bank of a
river. Out of nowhere, very quietly a boat appeared
and a man sat in it. He had paddles which hardly
made a sound. The people and my mother got into
it. That's all I remember. I must have fallen off to
sleep. I don't even remember getting out of the
boat. My mother said that when we did get off [the
boat] she stayed close to the river. We were safe
then, and across the river she saw a man leisurely
walking on the Russian side of the river. It was my*

uncle making sure we were safely across. They were saying good-by to each other.

Ita Pogrebiski

The Escape

My mother had very little memory of her life in
Russia. What she wrote in her first three chapters
was derived mostly from the stories she was told
later by her mother and siblings. Now, starting with
The Escape her memoirs are, for the first time, her
experience.

My mother was probably three, or at the most four,
at the time when she and her mother escaped from
Russia. My mother stated that her uncle came
along. It was not clear whether this male relative
was serving as guide and protector for the young
mother and her child, or if he was planning to join
them in their escape. Did his efforts fail because
there was not enough room in the boat for all three
of them? Or, did he sacrifice his place so they
could go? What is clear is he stayed behind in
Russia, and once my grandmother Shandel said
goodbye on the banks of the river, she never saw
this brother again.

My mother told me that for a while there was
correspondence between my grandmother and her
family left behind in Eastern Europe. This
continued even after they arrived in the United
States, and then at some point the correspondence
stopped. There were several possibilities for the
cessation. First, this may have been the result of
distance in miles and years between Shandel and
her family. Second, her relatives may have been

killed in the Holocaust. Sixty percent of the Jews living in the Ukraine, and fifty percent in Romania were murdered. Third, shortly after the end of World War II there was an anti-Communist witch-hunt going on in the United States. As a recent immigrant, did my grandmother fear mail coming to her home from a Communist country would be seen as un-American? My mother never said, but I know as an immigrant fleeing for her life, my mother saw life differently, and felt more threatened than someone who had only experienced a safe and peaceful upbringing.

The only anecdote my mother didn't include in her story of escape, which she told me many times, was about the bullets whizzing over her head. She was carried, by either her uncle or mother, and when they arrived at the Russian border, they were fired upon by border guards. In her child's mind she thought the bullets were noisy "toys," and tried to catch them with her outstretched arms.

The river that divided Russia from Romania was the Dneister (pronounced nee-ster). It is 846 miles long and has various names depending on the country it meanders through. In The Ukraine it is called Nistru; in Russia, Dniestr; in Poland, Dnister; in Romania, Dnister or Dneister. The Yiddish speaking Jews called it Nester. The river starts in the Carpathian Mountains and empties into the Black Sea.

My mother and her family chose to settle in Balti, Romania because they already had family living there. The distance between Balti and Kiev is approximately 300 miles. My mother never mentioned exactly how long it took to travel that distance or how it was done. She only mentions that they either walked or ran. If this distance was accomplished only by foot then it would have taken at least thirty days based on an average person walking ten miles a day. For my relatives, it probably took longer because they were hampered with a young child and the danger on both sides of the border.

While the life-threatening conditions my mother and grandmother were leaving behind in Russia were real, they were not naïve to think that Romania would welcome them with open arms and offer a life of tolerance and acceptance. Family that was already in Romania probably told them what to expect, and while it was not perfect, at least there were few pogroms. The one sad, but positive, note about their move was they were not strangers to this unkind environment and their survival instincts were finely tuned.

Jews have resided in Romania since the Roman occupation. Many more came in the second millennia either as a result of instability like the Khmelnytsky Uprising in the Ukraine in the middle of the seventeenth century, shifting boundaries before and after the World Wars, and immigration from Russia.

Most Jews resided in the province of Moldavia which was in eastern Romania, and by 1899 they were 4.5% of the total population. Starting in 1900 the number of Jews in Romania started to decline because of massive immigration to the United States. The first to leave were called *fusgayers*, "immigrants who left on foot," and were given assistance by various charitable Jewish organizations along their way to the west.

At first, Russian Jews were welcomed to Romania in the beginning of the nineteenth century, but by 1866 the constitution granted citizenship and full civil rights only to Christians. Only in the case of an exceptional ruling passed during Romania's participation in the Russian-Turkey War in 1877, were 888 Jewish soldiers granted citizenship. This ruling did not survive till World War I even though 25,000 Jews served and 882 were killed. However, during the same war 150 Jewish soldiers were condemned for treason or espionage for such infractions as speaking Yiddish on the front line. Therefore, without legal guarantees, discrimination and abuse was perpetrated by the government, the press and political groups. International intervention by American and Jewish agencies only increased the anti-Semitism. Not until the Treaty of Versailles in 1919, with the Minorities Treaties, was Romania compelled to grant full citizenship and ensure basic human rights to all. This took effect in 1923. My mother arrived in Romania around 1921.

Although Jews were denied civil rights they were allowed the freedom to make a living, and were solidly entrenched in the middle class. They worked as shopkeepers, money lenders, doctors, lawyers, and engineers. In the crafts they became the majority workers as watchmakers, hatters, platers, engravers, typographers, and bookbinders. In industry they were also the majority in the making of glassware, furniture, and textiles. At the turn of the twentieth century over one-fifth of all merchants and thirty-eight percent of all physicians were Jews. By this time several Jewish banks were successfully established as well.

There were two provinces in Romania. The larger was Walachia, also known as the old kingdom, and Moldavia, situated between the Ukraine and Walachia. Each had Jewish residents but the larger number lived in Moldavia. The Jews of Moldavia were Yiddish speaking, Ashkenazi Jews from Eastern Europe. They lived in rural communities such as a small market town or village. They tended not to assimilate and were more religious. On the other hand, the Jews of Walachia were Western European Ashkenazi (Germany and Austria) and Sephardic Jews. Sephardim (plural) could trace their ancestry to the exodus from the Iberian Peninsula during the Spanish Inquisition. The Jews of Walachia lived in large cities, were more likely to assimilate and accept modernization, rarely spoke Yiddish, but still maintained their Jewish identity. The Sephardic and Ashkenazi Jews of Walachia had separate synagogues, schools,

charitable organizations, traditions and
communities.

It did not matter if one was Ashkenazi or Sephardic
from Moldavia or Walachia, the attitude towards
Jews, as stated by historian Serban Papacostea, was
"hostile tolerance." With the lack of civil
protection they were often at the mercy when
hostilities broke out such as a pogrom in Galati in
1859 and an uprising of the peasantry in 1907.
After World War I, the Jews were considered
parasitic foreigners who infiltrated the economy and
were the reason most Romanians lived in poverty
and misery. Jews were accused of not wanting to
assimilate and therefore weakened Romanian
nationalism. There was a call for Jews to be barred
from economic life and that the young be re-
educated and infused with "Christian and
nationalistic spirit." Like Russia, xenophobia was
alive and well in Romania, and into this toxic
environment my mother and Shandel began their
lives in Balti, Moldavia, Romania.

Balti was the capital of Bessarabia which was part
of the province of Moldavia. The city is located
where several railroad lines converge and is next to
the Reut River, a tributary to the Dneister River.
The Russians, and probably my mother's family,
called the city Beltsy or Beltz. Depending on which
country was more powerful, control of Moldavia
and Bessarabia was tossed back and forth between
Russia and Romania. In 1918 Bessarabia passed to
Romania and thus when my mother arrived in 1921

she was on Romanian soil. Moldavia is the historical name for the province. Since 1991 it is the independent Republic of Moldova.

In 1921 approximately sixty percent of Balti's population was Jewish, the highest concentration of Jews in Romania. One of the reasons for this was the influx of refugees fleeing the pogroms and revolution in Russia. Starting at the end of the nineteenth century and continuing for the next twenty to thirty years, many Jews arrived in Balti at the same time many were leaving for the west so that from 1910 to 1930 the population remained steady.

The new Russian Jews who settled in Balti were educated, professional, and more enlightened, thus providing an interesting dimension to the already vibrant culture. This change extended to all areas of life in Balti: education, theater, music, literature, sports, and the economy.

At the end of the nineteenth century, Balti had only religious schools but when my mother arrived there were Jewish secular schools, Zionist schools, and a private school for boys. In addition, in 1918, a Jewish parents group was created and they formed an elementary school, a separate *gymnasium* (academic high school), one for boys and one for girls; kindergarten classes were started two years later. My mother attended school there.

The arts were alive and well in Balti. There was theater, both professional and amateur, an orchestra, and silent movies with live music was offered at the cinemas. Balti was on the circuit for traveling theater groups, internationally known professional actors, opera singers and musicians. The local theater and wind orchestra served as an incubator for future talent. Children were enrolled in music schools, and private lessons were offered in piano and violin. Some child prodigies went on to perform in world-class orchestras.

The citizens of Balti had access to various forms of literature. They had a large public library, as well as public collections of books written in Yiddish, Hebrew, Romanian and Russian. The Jewish *gymnasium* also had a large library. There were book stores and Jewish and Romanian printing houses, and a local paper and a literary journal. When the government decided to close down a Hebrew publication, the owner just renamed it and started publishing once again.

As in the Russian shtetl, the Jews set up the social welfare institutions. They created a hospital, a home for seniors, and collected charity for the poor. Job training was provided for poor children. This was established through organizations like ORT (Organization For Rehabilitation Through Training) which provided educational and vocational training at no cost. ORT continues to exist today.

As opposed to other areas of Romania, Balti was a good place for the Jews. Anti-Semitism was kept under control. This was partly due to the major role the Jews played in the economic success of the town and the Romanian government wanted to maintain that. The commander of the area was pro-active to ensure the peace, and additionally, there was a Jewish militia which helped to discourage troublemakers. Government officials included Jews when it came to local matters, and the Bishop of Balti, Viserion Puyu, donated money to the Jewish hospital. When he was made archbishop he donated even more as his farewell gift. These goodwill gestures did not solve all the problems, but for the most part the Jews and their Christian neighbors got along.

The peace continued through the 1920's. Anti-Semitic incidents were met with punishment for the guilty. By the 1930's, the Jews of Europe were in trouble and it was no different in Romania. Jewish homes were destroyed; a cemetery was desecrated. Jewish children were expelled from school and beaten up. Eventually, Jewish schools were closed down and the only way they could reopen was with a government approved curriculum. Jewish high school students were denied when they tried to be a part of a national event. These incidents became the stimuli for the resumption of pogroms. The mayor of Balti tried to intervene and asked for help from the government, but he was denied. By the beginning of World War II, once again Bessarabia, including Balti, was annexed by the Russians.

When the Romanians tried to reconquer Balti, they robbed, killed and raped thousands of Jews who were trying to escape. The Nazis advanced and along with the help of the Romanian army, Balti was conquered by the Germans on July 9, 1941.

Sherry V. Ostroff

Life in Romania

Like I said we seemed to have relatives all over and wouldn't you know it we had relatives in Romania too, in the little city of Beltz. Before I get any further, before mom and I got to Romania, my sister and brother got there first and when we arrived only my brother was there, as my sister, who was the eldest of my mother's children, was gone to America. My Uncle Julius, his wife, [his] little daughter, his wife's sister and brother and my sister Anna all brought over to America, all at the same time on the same boat. [My Uncle Julius] selected my sister because she was at an age where she could go to work in America and help to bring all three of us over.

So, now we lived in Romania. Our relatives [in Romania] were Uncle Moishe, who was studying to be a doctor, his wife and son. Then we had two great-great aunts who were sisters. They were very old and had long grey hair hanging down straight in their backs. They always wore long black capes, summer and winter. They looked a lot like two Miss Clavels from the children's story book [Madeline]. They were widows. One aunt had two daughters, one of which was an old-maid. This daughter's one and only love died, and she was heartbroken and didn't want anyone else (which broke her mother's heart). She taught Hebrew in school. The second daughter was married to a

101

teacher and had two children, but they lived in a different city in Romania. The other one of my great-great aunts also had two daughters. The older one was married, was well-to-do and had three teenagers. Her husband was a stock broker. The second daughter was a head nurse. Then we had other cousins and their children, so actually we were not alone in Beltz. But let me tell you that with all the relatives, if you are a widow you are alone.

We lived in one room [which had] one door that opened to a balcony facing the inside of a small court. All three of us, my mother, my brother and I [lived in this one room]. The toilet was [an] outhouse and we got water from an outdoor pump. The light was a kerosene lamp. In the room were two single beds, one for my brother and one for mom and me. [There were] two old wooden chairs and a small table. We never had a tablecloth, my mother use to cover the table with paper she got from the grocer.

At first I use to think my brother was my father. First of all, he seemed big like a man, and then he used to holler at my mother and last but not least he would beat me all the time especially when I used to wet the bed and he had to clean it up.

My mother tried to earn a few pennies so she would sit every day inside the Hebrew school hall and sell candies to the children. When I would wake up in the morning my mother was already gone to the school with her wares. Close to my bed stood one of the chairs with a bagel hang[ing] on the back piece of wood that stuck out. That was to be my breakfast, but I had a problem. If I reached for the bagel my brother, who slept across the room was waking up, and he would see that my bed was wet and that meant a lickin'. My plan was to make believe I was still sleeping and when he bent down to reach for his shoes I would grab for the bagel and run out of the room. His bed was near the door and I didn't always make [it]. This time I did, he scream[ed] and called me to come back, but I didn't listen. I ran straight to the school where my mother was. I rush[ed] through the school hall and the children burst out laughing because I wasn't fully dressed. All I had on was a little pretty coat but being innocent I did[n't] even know why they were laughing. Once again my mother opened up her shawl and put her arms around me and I was safe and she even let me eat a chocolate.

We also had a number of cousins in Romania. One cousin Jennie, whose husband worked in the stock market, had three daughters. The middle one was my age. [We] always had fun together and we used to visit them often. We had other cousins and always kept close.

My sister use to write to my mother every day from America. The letters came regularly like clock[work] and it was really amazing. Once a week [my mother] received money to live on. All of our relatives envied my mother and some thought she was rich.

For some reason or another we moved around constantly but always in just one room. Then all of a sudden my mother announced that my brother Jack was leaving, he was going to America. I was delighted, now I wasn't going to be hit anymore. Then it turned out he wasn't going for another half year.

My mother had to report to the police station and have to get her passport renewed. She had to do this because she was Jewish and she was from Russia. Many times I was left to fend for myself - sometimes the landlady took care of me because my mother couldn't take me with her.

At times [my mother] was told by a friend or relative there was going to be a raid in the street and they were going to round up the Russian Jews. At the news we left town and went to live in another town till things calmed down, then we would move back and live in a different one room apartment.

My Uncle Moishe who was studying said he couldn't continue studying in Romania because he was Jewish and the[y] wouldn't accept him in the particular college so he had to go to another country where Jews were acceptable. [He] and his wife and child moved to Prague, Czechoslovakia.

Every year my mother had to go to the capital city of Romania, Bucharest, to find out if she was on the list, the quota, to go to America. Sometimes she would have to stay there a week until she was able to see the right people to get the information. Usually, she went to the HIAS office, and I was taken care of by some friend while she was gone. I would cry constantly. Between the HIAS and the police station visitation, I did nothing but cry.

Passover and Easter which fell pretty close in dates, we used to go in hiding because the drunken Christians roamed the streets with their farmer tools, hammers and knives, tried to catch Jews in the streets and kill them. That was a constant fear.

If a prominent officer died in the city, and there was a big city funeral and procession to the church, the Jew better not be near or around them because some Christian would holler out there is that Jew, what is he doing here and he would [get] a beating.

One summer my great-great aunt and her daughter, my mother and I moved out (my brother had already left for America) of Beltz, to a nearby farm. [It was] a Christian [owned] farm and we had two bedrooms and a kitchen. The farmer had many kids and once I was asked to go out in the fields with the kids. [We] sat on top of a pile of hay.

I played all day in the fields while the older kids worked all day. We didn't get home till sunset.

One evening the farmer knocked on our door and asked if we wouldn't mind [letting] in a woman overnight and give her shelter. She ran away from her drunken husband's beatings. Quickly, my great-great aunt thought that if she was ever found hiding among us we would all be killed. The farmer said they would never think of searching in a Jewish home. My aunt said had we a man of the house she wouldn't hesitate taking her in, but since we were only women we were just as helpless and had no protection. The landlord said he understood our reasoning and said we were right. After that episode my relatives saw that one time or another we might get involved in a situation and get ourselves killed, so we moved back to the city.

Another time we lived with the same aunt in a second floor apartment. My mother was away most of the day. She was learning to be a milliner so when she ever went to America she would be able to get a job. My great-great aunt took care of me being she was so old and she not worrying very much about me, she let me be on my own a lot. I wandered the streets, took off my shoes, which I wasn't allowed to do, and walked in the mud and played with all the kids my mother told me not to play with. They were considered the children of the low class people. I went to their houses and innocently told their mothers that I wasn't allowed to play with their children, and I was doing it because my mother wasn't home and I wasn't going to tell her. I asked them not to tell her, and the mothers and children promised. Most of the mothers in my neighborhood didn't allow their children to play with the [low class] either. Now they were[n't] drunks or robbers or dishonest. They were shoemakers. They were common, unlearned and poor and kept their homes dirty and the children were dirty. But, I had such fun playing with them.

My great-great aunt would call me for dinner. I would rush home and put on my socks and shoes so the muck wouldn't show. She complained that I was always so dirty. Her daughter would come home from teaching and she would help me wash up. She kept constantly hollering and pinching me for getting so dirty and I would cry from the pain. By the time my mother came, I was clean and fed and looked like the nicest, [well-]behaved little miss.

There was a custom in Romania, weeks before Passover, matzah would be distributed from the baker to the Jewish families. The orders were carried through the streets by two men. A sheet was tied to two long poles by the corners and the men held the poles on their shoulder [so] that the matzah nestled in the center pocket of the sheet. That's how they delivered the matzah.

Passover was the delight of the Jewish people [except for the danger of pogroms) and

*especially for the little children. At that time my
great-great aunt and her daughter left us alone in
the apartment. She went to visit her other daughter
for the holiday. So, we, mother and I, were left
alone. (I think my great-great aunt asked my mother
to come along, but she refused.) It wasn't much
fun sitting, just us two, around the table. My
mother would put the matzahs on the table and the
candles, and the food. Also, she never failed to put
out my sister's and brother's pictures that were sent
to us from America, and then she started to cry and
cry, and then I started to cry because my mother
cried. But my mother cried so hard she became
hysterical and then she would drop into a faint and
I would start screaming and crying and running to
the next door neighbor telling them that my mother
died. I thought she was dead. They rushed in and
revived her. That is how we spent all of our
Passover holidays, crying and fainting. I can't
blame my mother considering the life she had in the
past compared to what she had now.*

*Beltz was a big town. It had a railroad
station down a steep street at the end of the town,
no buses or trolleys cars. The only other way to get
around was by horse, horse and wagon, horse and
buggy, bicycles, or walking. The main street was
paved but not the secondary streets, at least most
second streets were not paved, that meant when it
rained the secondary streets were muddy. There
was no city hall but there was a police station, a
post office and a large prison with a yard and walls
all around. The police patrolled the walls night and*

day and carried their guns all the time. [This] scared the little children and I never walked close to it. There was a great big beautiful church with big church bells and beautiful grounds and a fence around it. Believe me, that church was beautiful inside as one day I peeked through the door and it was magnificent. It must have been made with gold. It gleamed so. I had never seen anything so beautiful. Most large churches in Europe were beautiful.

There were no dress [or] men's clothing stores. If you wanted clothes you bought material by the yard and took it to the dressmaker or tailor and had it handmade. First, you would go to the dressmaker or tailor and pick your style from a fashion magazine. Then you got measured and then you bought your material. [For] shoes you went to the shoemaker, he made your shoes. There were no department stores or five and ten stores. The stores were small. They had some fruit stores in the center of town. They were very expensive. They had grocery stores [and] bakeries which were also expensive. They featured a lot of French pastries and cakes. It smelled so good just passing by. There were fancy dairy stores, book stores, toy stores, hardware, dry goods and candy stores, etc.

People did most of their buying at the bazaar. It was a big open area that was set aside for that purpose. Twice a week the farmers would come with their wagons loaded with all kinds of wares, set it up in stalls and tables and sell to the

*people. There, you could buy most anything: live
chickens, fish, geese, fruits of all sorts, (not
oranges, they were imported and only could be
gotten in specialty stores) grapes, pears, plums and
cherries, etc. [You could buy] vegetables of all
sorts and handmade woven rugs, wood chairs,
bowls, and trinkets. Most anything you would want.
[There were] lots of odd things. For everything you
had to bargain.*

*It would be easier to mention the foods that I
never saw in Romania. Most of these were the
tropical foods. Probably they were sold in the
specialty shops which I never walked into because
of the high prices. That was where only the rich
went. The fruit I never saw were bananas,
grapefruit, and oranges. [My] mother did buy [an
orange] in the specialty store. They were close to
the door because I was taking castor oil and she
bought one orange for me. The skin was saved and
dried, and we kept smelling it over and over again.
[I never] saw lettuce, celery or canned food. Milk
and dairy was brought to our house daily by the
farmers. Milk was always boiled before using.
Water was brought daily by a waterman who had a
barrel the size of huge tank on his wagon. This tank
size barrel had a hole in it with a wooden plug. He
would pull out the plug, hold a bucket under the
gushing water, fill it and replug the hole. He
carried the water to the houses that had ordered the
water. This was the drinking and cooking water for
the people in the city. It was boiled before using. It
also served [for] washing oneself.*

110

Some homes in Romania had dug out cellars or caves under yards or homes. They were deep and long and [this is where] people kept their stored food. It was cold just like a refrigerator. Sometimes these places were used as a hide-away.

In Beltz, Romania we kept moving from one apartment to another. When we returned from the villages we were forced to move elsewhere because our former apartment would be rented to someone else. This time we moved into a rich widow's apartment. She had a yard goods store in front. In the back of the store was a kitchen which we shared with her, then her bedroom and in the last room was a dining room in which was a sofa in which my mother and I slept.

One time I became ill. I don't really know what was the matter. All I remember is I was in a deep sleep. All of sudden I felt an ice cold thing set on my chest. I opened my eyes with shock and there was a doctor's cold ear on my chest. My mother was standing nearby. The doctor decided to apply leeches. I was really and truly frightened, but I was convinced it wouldn't hurt. [Instead] the doctor [took] from his suitcase threes glass cups [suction cups] that did not have handles like regular cups. He lights up a light with alcohol and swabs and heats the inside of the cup and when it is hot but not too hot to hurt, he applies it to [my] body till he put on as many as he want[ed]. The heat [is]in the [inside of the] cup and the air is shut off. The cup draws the flesh up and acts like a vacuum. After a *while the doctor pops them off, and you can see a round rim shows where the rim was and the inner puffy flesh is quite red. When these cups are left on the skin a long time, the flesh where the rim has been starts bleeding. That is what people use to do when they wanted to bleed a person in older times.*

One summer my mother again had to leave Beltz again because a raid on Russian Jews was rumored to take place soon. So we went away to stay in a small village. We stayed in a one room apartment in a small court, and next to us was another room occupied by a Jewish woman with two children. They were older than I but the boy was the younger of the two. I played with the boy all of the time. We did everything together. In the front part of the court was a large apartment facing the street. This large apartment was occupied by an officer and his wife. They had a number of soldiers in the apartment doing household duties: cooking, cleaning, taking care of [the] officer's shoes and boots, etc. Of course, they were all Christians including the landlord.

One time this other kid, I don't remember his name, and I were sent on an errand. On the way home we were each carrying a package. My friend said to me, [let's] see how muddy our shoes get. Then, we noticed in front of the officer's door there was a mat. My friend dared me to wipe my shoes on it and I took him up on his dare. Just then the soldiers' servant saw me I ran away. Of course, I never told my mother and in fact I had forgotten the incident completely. I felt since I ran away, and no one followed me I was safe.

A few days later my mother was away on an errand, and our Jewish neighbor and her two children were also away. I was alone. I tried to amuse myself and play different kinds of games. I had a broom between my feet and making believe I was riding a horse. I was neighing and going back and forth. As I was playing I noticed the officer was walk[ing] also back and forth and in his hand he was holding a horse whip. Since I knew there was no real horse around, I realized he didn't need the whip. Also, there was no one around but me, and somehow I got the feeling he intended to use the whip on me. I made believe I was still riding on the broom and I went into the room, locked the door, closed the shutters and stayed in the dark. I guess that officer wanted to whip me because I wiped my muddy shoes on his mat, but he didn't quite make up his mind, although he was tempted to do so. Only God in heaven saved me from that whipping. Of course, I never told my mother about that either.

Also, later the landlord's father died and he was laid out on the dining room table for friends and relatives to view. I peeped in and then walked in because no one was there. This was the first time I had ever seen a dead person. Then I went to our room and I asked my mother to show me my father's picture, and I cried like a baby.

My mother had never told me outright that my father was dead. For years she told me that he was in America with my sister. I believed her. Then I asked her why did Anna write letters to us [but] not my father. Then, my mother said, "Sure your father writes," and to prove it she took a paper and started to read. What she read sounded like sheer delight. Father said he loved me and missed me and kissed me, but then I noticed that there was no writing on the paper. I knew mother was making all this up.

Deep in my heart I walked around with envy of my cousins and girlfriends. They all had fathers and I didn't. Since I wasn't told the truth I thought that any man with a beard that I saw walking on the street might turn out to be my father. Sometimes I would call out, "Father, Father," figuring if it was my father he would answer. But no one answered my call and many a tear did I shed. But [I] consoled myself, maybe I will find him tomorrow on another street.

One time my mother left me home, kissed me good bye and went to do some shopping. When she returned, instead of greeting me, she gave me a great big lickin'. She never said why, and I couldn't guess. The only thing I could think of was somewhere she must have an exact twin. My good sweet mother was kidnapped by the gypsies and the wicked one [was] substituted for her.

Another time my mother had to go to the
headquarters' office of the HIAS which was located
in Bucharest, the capital city of Romania to find out
if we were going to be on that year's quota to go to
the USA. With another woman, my mother rented a
room, and this time I [was] to come along. Well,
just then I got the measles. I remember looking at
myself and seeing these little bumps all over me.
The woman we roomed with seemed always to be
out and my mother left me alone in this room as she
had to go to the HIAS.

The hours and days seemed dark and
gloomy when I was by myself, and then the roof
started to leak. My mother kept a pan under the
leak and it was always cold in there. The doctor
advised mother to look for another room, even
though we needed it only for two or three weeks.
This time we moved in another room by ourselves.
After the measles I had complications. The doctor
prescribed medication every 4 hours, day and night.
In the day my mother set the clock [that] told me
when to take the medicine. At night my mother gave
me the medicine, went to sleep, and then about an
hour or so woke up not remembering she already
had given me the medicine [and] gave it to me
again. Then some time later it occurred to her that
she had given me an overdose. She felt my skin and
I was as cold as a rock. She screamed and the
people surrounding us came running and someone
ran for the doctor in the night. He gave me an
antidote and told my mother this can't go on. He
wanted me to go to a hospital. He was going to

make arrangements through a friend that my mother was to stay in the hospital with the arrangement that my mother be an aide.

There we were in the hospital. I was in the children's ward. I saw little of my mother, only when [she] changed the beds, took the temperature or brought in the food trays. But, I knew mother was there and that was good enough for me.

Then one morning she said she had to go the HIAS and she would be back in the afternoon. It started to snow that day early in the morning. I kept looking through the hospital window. Afternoon came and went and it was later, no mother. I kept looking for her to come through the gates, as I could see them there through the window. [There] were wrought iron gates all around the hospital and the gates of the hospital were locked tight at four. They did not get opened until the next morning. It was going on three, and then four, and my mother did not show up. Then after five [I] looked out the window and saw a lone figure on the outside of the gates. Later the figure sat down on a bench outside the gate and thus sat till [the] next day in the cold and snow. I cried all thought the night. Of course, I pointed out my mother to the nurses and they couldn't do anything to get the gates opened.

Once before Passover mother scoured the water barrel to make it kosher of Passover. She heated some rocks over an open fire, placed them

116

into the barrel and poured hot water over them. The water sizzled from the heat and that made it kosher. Then the barrel was filled with fresh water that the water carrier brought.

This particular Passover my mother scoured the barrel and waited for the water carrier. Meanwhile, she went to do some shopping. I decided to help her, she seemed so busy since before each Passover everyone white-washed their kitchen walls. I decided to do that for her. Since there was no water in the barrel, I decided to use the next best thing. She had plenty of eggs set aside for Passover cooking, so I used them with a rag. I washed walls, furniture, [and] droppings [got on] the floor including myself. Guess how many pinches I got, plus a lickin' and a haircut.

The barrels of drinking and cooking water also served as a nice game for the children. When the parents were [not around], the children surrounded the barrel with stools. They stood on their tip toes and spit into the barrel to see who would make [the] biggest bubble. It truly was great fun.

One Passover my great-great Aunt Pessa Ruthil persuaded my mother and me to go along to a small village where her daughter lived and stay [with them] till after Passover. My great-great aunt and her daughter (that hadn't married) stayed with the daughter [from] the small village with her family. So, my mother rented a room for us. Just before Passover eve my mother bathed me in a laundry basin and she dressed me in my best dress, coat and new shoes and told me to go early by myself and she would come later on. I was so happy to have my best clothes on [and] couldn't wait till [my aunt and her daughters] saw me. The house was on the outskirts of the village and I proceeded to walk, but before I knew it I was in deep trouble. I walked in a mud puddle. I could hardly lift my feet up and when I took another step, flop and I fell down into the mud. I thought I would never make it as I kept falling over and over again. Finally, somehow I made it, showed up to the house. My aunt never hollered at me. She hushed up my crying, washed me in the laundry basin, and dressed me in my cousin's blouse which reached to the floor. She washed my dress, under clothes and my coat. I had lost my shoes. When my mother arrived everything was under control and we proceeded to have a Passover Seder.

That was the first time I had been [to] a real Passover Seder. It was so beautiful, cheerful and bright. I thought I was witnessing something that only occurred in heaven. It lasted and lasted what seemed till [the] wee hours.

My mother stayed longer that Passover in the village and I went to school there. One day while I was sitting in class, I was called to the office to see the principal. I was so frightened and couldn't imagine what I had done wrong. I imagined I was going to be arrested and put in prison. When [I] finally stood in front of the principal, shivering and shaking, the principal told me that this was the second week that my mother failed to pay for the tuition fee, and I was to go home. I said, "Okay," and started to go back to my class. He asked me where I was going and I said I was going to get my coat. He said I couldn't get my coat and I was to go home without it. So, I left to go home in the bitter cold. The school was in the outskirts of the village and I cried, walked and shivered. I walked and walked in the bitter cold wind. Finally, I reached where we lived. I cried but couldn't cry loud enough to make myself heard. Also, my hands were so cold I couldn't feel enough to lift my hands to knock on the door. It felt as if I didn't have any hands. A man passing by saw me and came over and asked me what was happening. I told him I was so cold I couldn't knock on the door. He knocked for me and the landlady heard him and she let me in.

There was a city public bath house which people used if they had the money. There were a couple of synagogues but they were small. On the days there was no bazaar, in that area where they were held, you could see some men making rope. They would spread out and stretch the straw that looked like fine fibers and stretched and twisted until it became long, strong and thin. It was sold wholesale to the hardware store to be sold retail. At other times, in this same area, the peasants bought big tubs and built a fire underneath. They made apple and plum butter to be sold. They cooked it right in front of your eyes.

There were some Hebrew schools and a public school. I went to the public school. Like it or not, every day you had to pray to Jesus, cross yourself and you also had to salute to the pictures on the wall that was the King of Romania. You had to do this or you were reported and they looked to see if your parents were an enemy of the country or a spy or a traitor.

There was a beautiful square park surrounded by an iron fence. To enter you had to go through turn stiles. There was no charge. The grounds were beautifully kept with walkways, gas lights, flowers of all sorts and benches to sit on. You were allowed to bring a lunch to the park but no cooking [was allowed]. They had a restaurant that you could eat inside or outside. But we never did because it was too expensive. This restaurant was located right along a circled walkway. In the exact center was a roofed stage where the band or orchestra played classical music and all kinds of marches. It was beautiful to see all the people come to stroll around, parents with their little children; lovers all dressed in their best enjoying themselves. It was so beautiful and cheerful. One felt like I wished never to have to leave this heavenly place.

Then there was a theater in town which I only went once. At times there were fireworks after the show late at night.

There was a movie house to which mother took me but once. It was a silent movie and it looked just beautiful. [The movie] showed people living in some kind of palace. I really wasn't able to get to know what was going on as my mother got sick and we had to leave.

Every spring covered wagons full of gypsies came to Beltz. They usually stayed on any empty plot of ground they could find. They sat on the bare ground, ate and cooked on their outdoor fires they built. Their children ran around barefoot and were dirty. The older gypsies looked dirty too. The younger ones wore those special gypsy skirts with a bolero, blouses, scarves with lots of colorful necklaces and earrings and they were also barefoot. Mother warned me never to go near them as not only were [they] dirty and some had lice, but they also kidnapped little children. Sometimes they asked for a ransom and sometimes they kept the children to increase their tribe.

As soon as the [gypsies] hit the town they had to report to the police station, get a permit to stay and to [indicate] how long they were staying. If they could afford it they could stay longer, but one thing for sure, towards winter they would be gone.

I mentioned that there was a post office in town. One time my mother mentioned that she had to go to the post office and she said I could go

121

along. She would show me that in the post office there was a wonderful new thing. It was in a little room and that [it] had a little box in it and you could talk into it. (the telephone) I remember walking with my mother towards this post office to see this wonder, holding onto her thumb, when I tripped and fell and scraped my knee and dirtied my dress. My mother pulled me up, scolded me, gave me a few pinches and I cried. She forgot to show me that wonderful little talking box.

I remember walking to school. I was in kindergarten. It was quite a distance as it was on the outskirts of the city. The streets were not paved and after a rain the mud was thick. I walked into it and the mud was so thick I couldn't move. I first lost one shoe and then the other. Then I couldn't lift my feet out of the mud to retrieve my shoes. I couldn't move and I started to cry. I don't know how long I cried but suddenly a youth saw my predicament and he walked right into the mud and lifted me out. I told him I was on my way to school. He told me to go to school as it was nearer than my home. So that day I went to school in bare feet. I don't remember how I got home that day. After the mud dried I looked for my shoes but I never found them.

Beltz was a pretty clean town. Most of the Jewish people lived in the town. They are the ones who owned the little shops. They were the tailors, dressmakers, the bakers, shoemakers, stockbrokers, bankers, lawyers and doctors. They were never the smithies, peddlers, water carriers, street cleaners or police. When a fire broke out the first thing people did was run to the churchyard and ring the church bell which could be heard all over the town, [even] the farmers on the outskirts. This alerted the volunteer firemen which was every man in town. Those people near the fire started to carry buckets of their drinking water till the water carriers came with their wagons which held those huge barrels that delivered drinking water in. The water carriers had to get the water from the water well. Most of the time a whole street of homes burned down until the fire was finally controlled. Fire was the feared dread of the people and when a fire broke out all differences and religions were forgotten and everyone helped each other.

If you had asked me at that time how God made rain I would have explained it this way. God had a bigger water barrel then the water carrier on a cloud and when God pulled the plug, it rained.

When it was rumored that the king or a high official was about to pass by on the street, on the way to some other destination, the city went crazy. The streets were washed and cleaned and streamers were hung street to street. Streets were roped off. Soldiers and officers were everywhere with full uniforms including swords and guns, ready to shoot anyone who so much as looked like they wanted to walk across where it was forbidden. Bands played for hours before the high official or king rode by. People were all over the place (except [in]

123

*forbidden area) in trees, [on] steps, roofs,
doorways, and balconies. It was beautiful and
exciting to see and be there, but at the same time it
was scary because of the military. You could feel
the tenseness of the citizens. If you kept your store
open for business you were in trouble, [considered]
a traitor and had to answer to the police for
questioning, so all the stores and schools were
closed tight. Everything was closed. You didn't
dare even give an opinion. You were there to cheer,
like it or not.*

*The same thing held true if an officer died.
Only then, his box was drawn by horse draped with
his uniform, hat and sword. All stores and schools
had to be closed and people were out on the street.
The church bells kept chiming (and boy was it loud)
for hours on end.*

*For the Jews those times were frightening
because they couldn't stay home. [They] had to
close the synagogues and stores and stay out on the
street to show his respect. Since most of the
[Jewish men] had beards, side [locks] and long
coats, they stuck out like sore thumbs. They were
often kicked, pushed and beaten, and the police and
military never saw anything. It was with a sigh of
relief when those parades and funerals were over.*

*If the officer who died was a Jew hater, the
Jews were in danger. If he had been a Jew
sympathizer, then the Jew was beaten because the
Christian didn't like the Jew to be liked.*

It was not uncommon to hear that at the train station or on the trains the Jewish passengers were beaten and beards were pulled. The Christians, including the peasants, shaved. Only the Christian priests had beards and those beards were long and they wore long black gowns to the ground with great big crosses around their necks.

In peaceful Romania the Jews lived on a time bomb. Anytime, anywhere they could be beaten, attacked or their businesses burned down or destroyed. That was their lot, and that was life in peaceful Romania.

Ita Pogrebiski

Life in Romania

My mother's life in Romania was not that benign.
Her mother was always concerned because they
were illegal immigrants. Being that my mother was
a child she didn't know any better, adult worries did
not concern her. She described her life in this new
country with the concerns of a child, going from
one escapade to the next, always seeming to find
her way into mud puddles and receiving many
pinches due to her mishaps. She described the
constant moving more as an adventure. She met
new relatives, made new friendships, and became
acquainted with different people.

One of those unusual groups was the gypsies.
When I was a child her tale about the gypsies was
one of my favorites. Unfortunately she didn't
include all of it in her written manuscript. She
mentioned that her mother warned her not to play
with the gypsy children as they were considered
dirty and the adults would resort to kidnapping. I
do not know if my grandmother made the threat up
to ensure my mother would listen to her, but it
didn't work. My mother made friends with a little
gypsy girl and enjoyed her company. They would
play dolls together, and my mother had a large
collection of handmade doll clothes. This was all
made by Shandel. One day, after playing with the
gypsy girl, the doll clothes were gone, and instead
my mother received a head full of lice. Shandel did
not have a special soap to get rid of the lice.

Instead, she cut my mother's hair very short and her scalp was rubbed with kerosene to kill the nits. One can only imagine how that smelled, but it did the trick and the lice was gone.

My mother also wrote about how the doctor cared for her when she was sick. He wanted to bleed her and there were two methods, leeches and cupping. There are two types of cupping, dry and wet. Her doctor used dry. Cupping was developed originally by the Egyptians and the Chinese. It was believed that it was an effective means to rid the body of dangerous toxins which caused the patient to become sick. If you got rid of the toxins, the patient had a better chance of being cured. The procedure involved creating a vacuum inside the glass cup. This was done by placing a piece of alcohol soaked cotton into the cup and then igniting it. The fire would consume any oxygen in the cup. Once the fire was extinguished the cup was quickly inverted onto the skin. The vacuum in the cup would suck in the skin after it was left on for a few minutes. Once the cup was removed my mother said her skin was red and started to bleed. The skin got red because of the expanded blood vessels. In some cases, a doctor might puncture the skin to promote the bleeding in an effort to reduce the toxins. Today, wet or dry cupping is used as an alternative method to traditional medicine, and there is no data about its effectiveness.

While in Romania my mother described the first funeral she attended. It was in fact a wake, because she said the body of the landlord was placed on a kitchen table and the mourners could come by and pay their respect. This was not a Jewish funeral. Jews do not have wakes nor do they have viewings before burial.

The objectives of a Jewish funeral are to respect the deceased and provide as much support for the grieving family as possible. The deceased is prepared by a sacred society of volunteers called *Chevra Kadishah*. During the preparation prayers are said, the body is ritually washed, and then dressed in a shroud. Women do this for a deceased woman; men do it for a man. Another function of the *Chevra Kadishah* is to never leave the body alone until the time of burial. This is to show respect for the soul of the deceased, and in the past it was ensure that no rodents or insects desecrated the body.

Together with the family, the *Chevra Kadishah* plan the funeral and what comes after. Funerals happen quickly, usually within a day or two, unless time is needed for a relative who has a distance to travel. Since the funeral is the most difficult part, the idea is to get it done, so that the family can begin mourning, and the healing process can start.

At the funeral the body is never on display, it is always in a closed coffin. There are no flowers. The reasons for this are simple. In the past, flowers were placed around to hide the smell of the decomposing body. Since Jewish funerals occur shortly after death, flowers are not necessary. Additionally, beautiful flowers can be a way to cover up the bleakness and sorrow felt as a result of losing a loved one. The Jewish way of thinking is the death should not be covered up but accepted and exposed for what it is. The better to accept the harsh reality so that healing can begin. Instead, mourners are encouraged to give to charity, usually one that is preferred by the family, rather than spend money on flowers.

Once the burial is over, the mourners return to the home of a relative for a meal of consolation. The meal is prepared by friends and family never by the grieving family. All relatives and friends are invited and this is the beginning of *Shiva*, a formal mourning period directly following a funeral. Friends and family come by the *Shiva* house to keep the mourners company so they are not left alone to deal with their grief. *Shiva* can last up to seven days but ends once the Sabbath begins.

The mourning period continues for eleven months and the family is expected to attend synagogue services and say a prayer for their deceased relative. Three to twelve months after the burial, a headstone is placed on the grave with a short ceremony called an unveiling.

My mother followed all of the Jewish burial traditions, but she had a few more customs that she and her family followed. When visiting a *Shiva* house, my mother would always bring a dessert.

The reason for this was since so many people would be visiting and paying their respects, the grieving family should not have to worry about food for everyone. Also, my mother would do what she could for the mourners. She would not allow them get their own food, instead she would serve them. She told me that mourners needed to be cared for. Lastly, I remember when my Aunt Anna died, *Shiva* was held at my mother's home. At one point my mother announced she was going for a walk by herself. She told me that a mourner needed some time for consolation on their own, and that this was part of the tradition she had learned from Shandel.

***

Coming to the United States was not a simple matter especially for immigrants coming from Eastern Europe. My mother and Shandel spent six years in Romania waiting for approval from the United States government to resume their journey west. The wait was never due to lack of funds because my mother's sister Anna was already earning an income in New York City, and she sent money regularly to Romania to pay for day-to-day living expenses and all travel costs. Because of Anna's obligation to save her family, she never had children. My mother told me that in the 1920's a pregnant woman would often have to leave her job, and Anna needed to work. Therefore, the only issue that delayed the departure of my mother and Shandel was the hostile atmosphere in Congress and throughout the country regarding immigration and foreigners.

Starting in 1880, and for the next fifty years, 23.4 million desperate immigrants poured into the United States. During this same time period Congress responded by passing at least fifteen restrictive immigration laws, each one shrinking the welcome mat until it almost disappeared. This legislation was so effective that for the ten year period from 1930-39 the number of immigrants allowed entry was reduced by 90%. The rise of Nazism, however, saw an increase of refugees all frantically trying to squeeze through a closing door.

The purpose of the new legislation was not only meant to cut down on the number of immigrants, but to control who was being allowed to enter. For example, in May 1882, the Chinese Exclusion Act was the first law of its kind that denied free and open immigration to all. This was followed three months later with further restrictions for individuals deemed as "lunatics," "idiots," and those "likely to become a public charge," namely foreign single women. A single woman with no references and little English might have difficulty finding work, and what work she would find was at starvation wages. The image of a working single woman was not in sync with what was considered the appropriate female lifestyle in the last quarter of the nineteenth century, the American Gilded Age. A woman was expected to be a wife and mother and her husband, her legal guardian, provided protection for her. Without that safety net, it was believed, the single female would end up on the public dole.

The Immigration Act of 1891 introduced health inspections and increased the categories of undesirables. The Immigration Bureau was granted the authority to deny entry to any newly arriving refugee who was deemed ill, mentally defective, or impoverished. Polygamists and convicted felons were also rooted out. While the idea of health screenings seemed a proper way to keep contagion controlled, it also became another tool to put undesirables back on the boat for a return trip.

Fifteen years later, three regulations were put into effect. First, the Immigration Act of 1906 disallowed entry to anyone who had tuberculosis, was mentally disabled, or a child who arrived without a guardian. Second, the Expatriation Act forced an American woman to lose her citizenship if she married a foreigner, and she was forced to become a citizen of her new husband's country. This was changed a decade and a half later and was in effect only if she married an Asian. Third, there was a Gentleman's Agreement between the United States and Japan. The terms were the US agreed not to publicly deny entry to Japanese citizens, and the Japanese government would do all it could to block its citizens from leaving.

Further restrictions were placed on Asians and others. The Immigration Act of 1917 barred all Asians, alcoholics, stowaways, vagrants, and epileptics. The entry tax was increased to discourage refugees, and a literacy test was now required for all over sixteen years of age so illiterates could be identified. The test was not effective, as a means to deny entry, because it was given in the native language. President Wilson tried to veto this act but his veto was overridden by Congress.

All of the restrictive legislation to this point was part of the opening act. Lack of widespread public outrage limiting Asian immigration, which mainly affected only the west coast, allowed government officials to move their policies forward, and now new groups were under attack.

In the early 1920's, new laws limited immigration from certain areas of Europe, namely the southern and eastern parts of the continent, where most Jews and Italians originated. The first law, the Emergency Quota Act, set the quota at 3%, and it was based on the number of American citizens and their country of origin listed in the 1910 census. For example, if there were 800,000 Americans of Russian descent living in the United States in 1910, then 24,000 Russians per year would be granted entry. President Wilson opposed the act with the pocket veto, but new President, Warren Harding, signed it into law. There was no restriction for citizens of Western Europe.

The Quota Act was replaced with the National Origins Act of 1924. The new guidelines further reduced the quota rate to 2% and changed the look back to the census of 1890. Why the change of census? There were a lot fewer immigrants from Eastern and Southern Europe living in the country in 1890, therefore drastically reducing the number of refugees. If there were 100,000 Americans of Russian descent listed on the 1890 census, then there were only 2,000 slots available, thus the notion that America was a melting pot was over. The quota stayed in effect until 1965.

The result of the second quota act was twofold. First, it increased the number of slots for countries that had very few wishing to leave. Then, it decreased the number of immigrants from parts of Europe where there were many begging to get out. The doors were open wide for some and slammed shut for others.

Immigration Quotas 1925-1927

Northwest Europe and Scandinavia		Eastern and Southern Europe		Other Countries	
Country	Quota	Country	Quota	Country	Quota
Germany	51,227	Poland	5,982	Africa (other than Egypt)	1,100
Great Britain and Northern Ireland	34,007	Italy	3,845	Armenia	124
Irish Free State (Ireland)	28,567	Czechoslovakia	3,073	Australia	121
Sweden	9,561	Russia	2,248	Palestine	100
Norway	6,453	Yugoslavia	671	Syria	100
France	3,954	Romania	603	Turkey	100
Denmark	2,789	Portugal	503	Egypt	100
Switzerland	2,081	Hungary	473	New Zealand & Pacific Islands	100
Netherlands	1,648	Lithuania	344	All others	1,900
Austria	785	Latvia	142		
Belgium	512	Spain	131		
Finland	471	Estonia	124		
Free City of Danzig	228	Albania	100		
Iceland	100	Bulgaria	100		
Luxembourg	100	Greece	100		
Total (Number)	142,483	Total (Number)	18,439	Total (Number)	3,745
Total (%)	86.5	Total (%)	11.2	Total (%)	2.3

(Total Annual immigrant quota: 164,667)

Why was the American government so concerned about immigration and persevered so assiduously for the exclusion of certain ethnic and racial groups? The answer is multi-layered and included various elements of American society from the 1880's to 1925. Each played a part: the economy, labor unions, pop culture, politics, ideology, intolerance, panic and nativism.

Whenever there was a downturn in the economic cycle, people looked for a scapegoat to explain lost jobs and bad times. This held true when a three year depression descended on the United States in 1882. Complaints came from labor unions like the 700,000 member strong Knights of Labor to eliminate the flow of competing cheap workers from other countries. American manufacturers wanted to increase profits, but the Knights argued that this lowered wages for all. A law was passed in 1885, and business owners could no longer import immigrants.

The Haymarket Riot in 1886 also heightened the fear about radicalized foreigners when workers in Chicago held a peaceful rally demanding better working conditions. The police tried to break up the rally, and the situation deteriorated quickly. A bomb was thrown at the police, they responded by opening fire, and eleven rioters and policemen were killed. Since the labor organizers were German immigrants, panic spread throughout the country about the alien menace.

Four years later, Boston's Immigration Restrictive League was founded. This privileged group called for an immigration policy based on ethnicity. Given the choice, they preferred the United States to be populated with enlightened and modern-thinking immigrants from Western and Northern Europe rather than the primitive, archaic and destitute people from Asia and Southern and Eastern Europe.

In 1901, President William McKinley was assassinated by a Polish- American, Leon Czolgosz. He was not an immigrant but his parents were, and that was enough to heighten American xenophobia. Congress responded by passing the Anarchist Exclusion Act which kept anyone who was considered a political fanatic out of the country.

There were popular books written on the subject of ethnic and racial superiority and purity. One, by Woodrow Wilson, written in 1902 was entitled, *History of the American People.* He described immigrants from Italy, Hungary and Poland as low class, stupid, mean, and lazy. He also blamed the governments of countries located in Southern Europe of trying to get rid of these troublesome citizens by unloading them on the shores of the United States.

Another author tried to use science for making the case for racial superiority. In 1916 eugenicist Madison Grant published his book called *The Passing of the Great Race in America.* The book was wildly popular and went through several printings. Grant claimed that the Anglo-Saxon race in America was superior, and their gene pool would be contaminated if they comingled with the inferior immigrants from Eastern and Southern Europe. Grant called for restricted immigration and a ban on marriage between the races. His work was embraced by Hitler who called Grant's book his bible. In reality it was pseudo-science racism and it was not till the 1930's when the country was engulfed with the Depression and the rise of Nazism that Grant fell out of favor with the American people.

Some members of the press fed Americans a daily or weekly dose of bigotry. It may have been a chance to sell more papers or provide a sounding board for the views of the owner. Henry Ford's weekly newspaper, the *Dearborn Independent,* gave him a platform to his 700,000 subscribers in the 1920's. He railed against what he called, the International Jews. He blamed them for all the ills of society from the downfall of the US economy to the lessening of American morality. He accused them for the start of World War I. Hitler welcomed Ford's views and some made their way into Nazi propaganda. Ford's paper was not the only rag to print anti-Semitic articles. Newspapers and magazines all over the country did so. They published articles and included political cartoons that portrayed the stereotypical Jew as controlling the banks and responsible for civil unrest. As a result, Jews, including American born, were denied professional employment and rejected from prominent universities and country club membership. In some towns, new laws were passed barring Jews from purchasing land or a home.

All of these influences swayed the American public and they required the government to do something about the threatening hordes of immigrants. Their so-called patriotic cry was for the salvation and preservation of America for Americans, to be insular and embrace nationalism and bar any who would put American ideals in jeopardy. Just as my mother and Shandel were trying to get their travel documents in order, the torch light on Lady Liberty was growing dimmer.

A.   Mitchell Palmer was Attorney General under Wilson. He was accused of not going after foreign radicals.
In this cartoon, he is seen as not protecting Americans (behind him) from the Jews who are stereotyped with beards and large noses. Palmer was a Quaker from Pennsylvania and he and his family were threatened and almost killed on several occasions by those who saw him as a threat to the American way of life.

***

While it was becoming increasingly difficult for refugees to enter into the United States, more than ever they needed assistance in their countries of origin to navigate their way through the bureaucratic maze of paperwork, the quota system, and the ever-changing immigration laws. My mother described in her story how Shandel had to leave her many times, either alone or with a relative, so she could go to the HIAS headquarters. HIAS stood for Hebrew Immigrant Assistance Society.

Originally HIAS was not an international agency. It started in 1881 in New York City by American Jews who were concerned about the plight of the huge number of their brethren fleeing the pogroms in Russia. At the time, caring for the immigrant was not the responsibility of the federal government, and so it was often left to reformers like Jane Addams who founded a shelter in Chicago called Hull House for the impoverished immigrant. The founders of HIAS were of like mind and offered similar services. They aided the New York bound immigrant with the basic necessities: food, shelter, clothing and a job. For those traveling to other cities, they provided train tickets. Later, they renovated a building and added classes for vocational training, a playground, dormitories, kosher kitchens, and a synagogue.

The HIAS expanded their reach and established a headquarters at Ellis Island and helped the new arrivals negotiate the intake process. They provided translation services to aid with medical screenings, professional defense for those who were in danger of being deported needlessly, provided guaranteed jobs, and if needed, the money necessary to pay the $25 fee to enter the United States.

In one case, in 1917, HIAS was able to save almost 600 refugees from being deported due to lack of funds or sponsors. HIAS located the support and most were allowed to remain. HIAS did whatever it took to keep the immigrant from being deported.

Fortunately, for my mother and my grandmother, HIAS expanded once again, and became a worldwide organization in 1921 just as they were arriving in Romania. They set up branches in foreign countries where Jews were waiting to emigrate. In this way they could guide the refugee through the entire process till they set foot on American soil and could survive independently. Thousands of refugees have relied on the services of HIAS, and many probably owe their lives to the organization.

HIAS still exists today. Their motto is, "Welcome the Stranger, Protect the Refugee." They continue to provide help to all refugees in trouble no matter what their ethnicity or religion. They are the only resettlement organization representing the United States in Europe and are currently involved with resettling Syrian refugees and Iranian minorities all over the world. They advocate the improvement of immigration policies worldwide which have become restrictive once again, although the need has increased. The present day situation is *déjà vu* to my mother's experience, which can only make us realize the truth imbedded in the statement, "Those who do not learn history are doomed to repeat it."

Sherry V. Ostroff

Political cartoon from 1921. It was called "The Only Way To Handle It."

Coming to America

When I was eight years old finally we were able to come to America. All of our European relatives and friends considered us lucky that we would at last be living in a free country, in the wonderful golden country, [the] United States of America.

Saying good-by wasn't easy but it was a great relief to leave this country, especially for my mother. She was going to America, the free country that was good to Jews. She was going to her two children, her brother and his family.

She baked for weeks and kept [it] hidden. [This was] in case she couldn't eat the food on the boat. My mother made strudel which could keep for weeks and other goodies which she packed in a wicker made trunk.

[On our way to the ship] we passed through Germany by train and through other countries and never stayed anywhere overnight. In France we stopped and joined another group going to America. [We] and this group stayed in Paris a couple of days in a small hotel which looked like a large boarding house. There was a small restaurant there with waiters. The food was so delicious and different. I felt like I could stay on forever. My mother told me what a great city Paris was, but I really saw little of it. The streets were *beautiful; the stores were big and magnificent. We didn't really go to see anything [because] we were not staying long enough. We couldn't speak the language.*

The group always stayed together. [There were always] at least two adults together. Women never walked alone. So my mother and I were always accompanied by this man from the group and he didn't know the language either. We had great difficulty with money, prices and change.

We did manage to get into a great big department store, the first for my mother and me. She bought a beautiful golden colored bed spread for my sister as a gift. [She also bought some] Coty Tea perfume, undiluted, of which even the bottle after it got used up, smelled heavenly for years.

From Paris we went by train to Cherbourg which is situated on the northern shores of France. There we were to get on a steamship to go to America. In Cherbourg, we had to wait a week till the ship would come in. There again, we stayed in a small boarding house with a restaurant. The restaurant really amazed me because my mother didn't have to cook and she didn't have to take out the strudel from the wicker basket.

Cherbourg was a small town and a few blocks away was the ocean. What amazed me the most [when I was staying there] was the sink and the spigot with the running water. I tried to trace where the water was coming from. It seemed to be coming right from the wall of the building. But how did it get into the wall of the building? More than likely, [it came] from the ocean. I figured at high tide it hit the wall and that only happen at night when I was sleeping. It never occurred [to me] that my mother might know, and I never asked her.

Before getting permission to get on board the ship to go to America, all the paper work was looked at, examined and signed. We had to get a physical. The doctor examined us, [would looked at our] eyes for disease and the body for other diseases. Finally, everyone had to be cleaned and sprayed for lice whether it was necessary or not.

Finally the boat arrived but it was not the boat that was to take us to America. That ship was too large to come to the coast line. So, we boarded a steam boat that took us out to sea. By then, there were many passengers going to the same place. Not only that, there were many more boats heading to the [larger] steamship [of the] White Star Line that was going to take us to America. That's what it was called, The White [Star] Steamship Line.

They put out a gangplank for the people to go on from the smaller boat to the steam ship. [The gangplank] consisted of a heavy cloth canvas with hardly a railing to hold on to. My mother held my hand and wouldn't you know it, my foot found a hole or opening and [I] went right through it. My mother had to pull me out and of course, I got plenty of pinches.

The steam ship was big and modern and beautiful. It had two large restaurants, ballrooms, dance rooms, orchestras, night clubs, balconies, lounge chairs on the deck, swimming pool, and a theater. Electric lights were everywhere. Elevators [were] something I had never seen before. The elevators were my heaven and the elevator [man] didn't mind having [me] on it at all, so I kept riding on it as long as I could.

In the dining room we had trouble [because] we couldn't read the menu. So, we had to be rude and point at the food [as] the waiters passed by with their trays. We only pointed at food we were familiar with. We were afraid of the fancy food as we didn't know what it was and we might not like it or the waiter might refuse to bring it. We didn't know we could order anything we wanted on the menu.

After the first day at sea my mother got sea sick and spent most of the time in the cabin. I was on my own in the dining room. Here I was seated at a large round table with dishes, silverware, tablecloth and napkins all by myself with a large menu and a waiter. I only pointed to the food I saw pass by on trays so all I ate was eggs. I was afraid to point to anything else.

148

*We had a nice, clean, well-furnished cabin.
A man was assigned to take care of us and give us
anything we wanted. A doctor came to see how my
mother was. Since he couldn't tell me that she was
sick with seasickness I thought she was surely going
to die. I had been sea sick only the first day. My
mother was seasick till we reached the shore, then
as if by magic she was well again.*

*We couldn't ask the [room steward] for
anything or [take advantage] of the luxurious things
because of the language barrier. We even had
trouble to ask about the bathroom. My mother
wanted me to point out, on myself since I was a little
girl, but I refused. But mother managed to point on
me and he understood.*

*My mother got acquainted with a man who
had his cabin across ours and he was Jewish. He
was well-to-do and must have been a sports man
because he wore knickers. We had never seen
knickers before and [we] called him The Man with
the Funny Pants. He happened to hold an orange
in his hand and when I asked where he got it, he
asked if I wanted [it]. My eyes must have shown
delight and he threw it to me. Thereafter, every day
he threw or rolled an orange on the floor toward me
and my mother and I were delighted [with the]
oranges, and in the winter time. Our trip to
America was in December.*

*Then, a special Christmas party was given
and I was invited even though I was Jewish. My*

149

mother told [me] I could go. There were a lot of children [there], [some] older than I, some younger and some my own age. We had goodies to eat and then all of a sudden there was a "Ho, Ho, Ho." We saw this giant of a man all dressed in red up with a pack on his back. It was scary. The children cried from fear and I too was scared. I had to hold in my tears so I could detect if he was going to hurt anyone. I had never seen a real live Santa Claus. In fact, I only saw a picture of a Santa once or twice and even then I had paid little attention to it.

Then this [Santa Claus] started to do [this] wondrous thing. He gave out toys and games which you could keep forever and take home. I was wishing for a doll but he gave me a great big set of water colors which I kept for many years and enjoyed immensely. I had never had water colors before, not even crayons or a book to drawn in. But at that time, I was disappointed because I didn't get a doll.

We traveled for eight days. We were one day late arriving in America because of storms and choppy waters. On the last day my mother felt better. We dressed and got in line for the doctor to look us over and see if we were well enough to go ashore. I got my cheeks pinched by my mother so I should look healthy. We passed inspection.

Then we stood on deck and saw the Statue of Liberty. It was a sight to behold. It seemed like a beautiful goddess and many people thanked God.

My mother tried to explain the significance of it and I understood only a little of what she explained. She said a little prayer and told me to join in. We thanked God from the bottom of our hearts that at last we were in America.

Ita Pogrebiski

Coming To America

My mother and grandmother traveled by steamship from Cherbourg, France to New York City. My mother mentioned to me there was another stop along the way, and it was probably Southhampton, England because that was the usual route before the ocean crossing. She also told me they traveled as second class passengers for one important reason. First and second class travelers did not have to go through the medical screenings at Ellis Island. Instead, the public health officials came on board the ship to inspect the passengers. It was done with civility and privacy as opposed to third class and steerage passengers who had an entirely different experience. They were herded off the ship, lugging their possessions, and stood in long lines often described as cattle chutes. If there was a health issue, a chalk mark was scrawled on their clothes so that everyone knew there was a problem. The immigrant had no idea what the mark meant, they just knew it was not good news. For the lower class passengers it was an embarassing and demeaning process and filled with apprehension.

The entire health screening procedure was adversarial. The immigrant who might have had a condition to conceal, like a withered arm or a rash, would do their best to hide it, while the public health official did their best to uncover it.

The feared screening was known by the immigrants before they set out on their journey. They were inspected before they got on the ship, and organizations like HIAS prepared would-be travelers what to expect when the they reached their destination. Maybe it was HIAS who suggested to my grandmother she should purchase second class tickets to avoid the harsher screening conditions at Ellis Island. Apparently, it worked for my mother and grandmother, because they came on shore without incident, met up with my Aunt Anna, and started their lives anew.

The ship my mother and grandmother traveled on was the *SS Majestic* of the British owned White Star Line. Originally, the *Majestic* was not British at all, but German, and it's original name was the *Bismarck*. The *Bismarck,* and two German sister steam ships, and were built to rival the British steampships of the White Star and Cunard Lines. That was not meant to be due to a provision in the Treaty of Versailles after World War I. *Bismarck* was part of Germany's war reparations, and was handed over to the British. Her maiden voyage was from Southhampton, England to New York on May 10, 1922. This remained her itinerary for much of her sailing lifespan. It is indeed a twist of fate that a German made ship was used to relocate thousands of Jewish refugees from harm's way.

A consequence of sailing on the *Majestic,* in the 1920's and early 1930's, was it became part of the infamous "booze cruises." As long as the ship was in international waters, the restrictions of American Prohibition did not matter, and the alcohol flowed. Occasionally, the *Majestic* would set sail for three days cruises to nowhere; the sole purpose of which was to escape the 18th amendment. These cruises were not marketed that way, but it was a part of the underground to circumvent the law just as much as speakeasies.

The *Majestic* was the largest ship in the White Star line, and at the time my mother sailed on her she was the largest ship in the world. The ship held that title till 1935. Eventually she was sold to the Cunard Line, and then to the British Admiralty where she was utilized for cadet training and renamed for the third time as the *Caldedonia*. In July, 1943, she was scrapped in Inverkeithing, Scotland.

My mother wrote in her story about Shandel making lots of strudel, enough to fill a wicker trunk, to take on the voyage. My mother told me there were two reasons her mother did so even though the ship would have more than enough food for them to eat. First, strudel would last a long time and it did not need refrigeration. It was filled with dried raisins, walnuts, sugar and cinnamon; it was the power bar of its time and perfect for travel. Second, my mother and grandmother kept kosher and they had no idea what food would be available for them to eat on the ship. They were both orthodox Jews, as were almost all the Jews in Europe, and they were not going to give up their religious dietary restrictions just because they happened to be on a ship. That was the reason why they ended up eating mostly eggs and fruit. The eggs, my mother told me, were hard boiled still in their shells. The oranges, she ate, had to be peeled. Because these two items were not exposed to any other food, they were acceptable to eat. While reminiscing shortly after writing her story, my mother remarked how the food issue was quite ironic. She and her mother had all this delectable food on the ship at their disposal, anything they could possibly wish for, but instead lived on eggs, oranges, and of course, strudel.

So what were these dietary restrictions that observant Jews follow? The laws for what is and what is not kosher (fit or proper) is stated in the Torah. The rules have been further explained and expanded by rabbi-scholars throughout the centuries, especially when a new food like margarine is introduced or a new invention like a dishwasher shows up.

At times, people have tried to rationalize the rules, and make some sense of it that squares with our modern take on things. Some have thought that the rules of keeping kosher were created out of some ancient health concern. For instance, by not consuming pig meat it was noted that Jews did not contract trichonosis whereas the non-Jewish population did, at least until it became common knowledge that pork had to be thoroughly cooked. There might be some truth to that reasoning, but it is fact that the USDA does not inspect kosher butchers and slaughterhouses because the kosher requirements far exceed the government's. However, if you ask a Jew why they do not eat pork, the reason is plain and simple, the Torah forbids it.

In the kosher world of cooking, food is divided into three categories: meat, dairy and pareve. Pareve food is neither meat nor dairy but can be eaten with either. Fruit, vegetables, nuts, flour, sugar, fish, and grains are examples of pareve food. If any of these are mixed with dairy or meat they are then considered meat or dairy.

What makes meat, "beasts of the earth," kosher, and not *treyf* (not kosher) is based on the description found in the Torah, Leviticus 11,3; Deuteronomy 14.6. The animal should have a split hoof and chew its cud. This category includes cattle, sheep, goats and deer. If the animal only has one attribute, like the non-cud-chewing pig with its split hoof, it is prohibited. In addition, chicken, geese, duck and turkeys are allowed; birds of prey are not. Fish that have fins and scales are kosher: salmon, tuna, carp, and herring. Shellfish are not. Reptiles, rodents, amphibians and insects are *treyf*. In addition, none of the organs, the eggs and the milk of forbidden animals are allowed. For instance, jello made from gelatin derived from pig marrow is not kosher.

How the animal is slaughtered and then prepared also plays a role in whether it is kosher or not. The animal must be killed in a humane manner. The knife used in the process must be razor sharp with no jagged edges so death is quick and painless. The method of slaughter, by a trained butcher (*shochet*), must be done in one clean stroke across the carotid artery. If the animal is caused any pain, it is declared *treyf*, and the meat is sold to another butcher.

Another reason for slaughtering the animal in this way is to allow for the blood to be drained quickly and completely. Jews are not permitted to eat the blood of any animal. For instance, care is also taken when using raw eggs. The kosher baker will crack open one egg at a time, in a separate bowl, and if a blood spot is found the egg is discarded. The reason for this abhorrence of eating blood is based on the belief that the "life of the animal is contained in the blood."

There are other reasons why some animals are not considered kosher. If any abrasions, injuries or evidence of disease is found, the carcass is sold to other butchers. In some cases, a postmortem examination of the lungs is also done, and if there are adhesions, the meat is sold to other butchers. Some parts of the cattle, like the sciatic nerve are not permitted for consumption. Because it is difficult and expensive to remove, the entire hindquarters of the cattle are sold to other butchers.

In order to make sure that food manufacturers package and correctly label the contents, there are specially trained rabbis who monitor the process. Many mistakenly believe that the rabbis are there to bless the food. That is not the case. They are there as kosher food inspectors to ensure that the consumer is getting a genuine product. If a food label is listed as non-dairy pareve, the contents are guaranteed not to have any trace of dairy in all of its various forms including whey, lactose, curds, and casein. In addition, the food cannot be prepared in machinery that once contained dairy. Non-dairy pareve means just that, and the same care is taken regarding meat.

Food preparation is also what makes food kosher. Dairy and meat products are never eaten or mixed together. This prohibition is based on the Torah and the lesson it teaches, is not to "boil a kid in its mother's milk." Some have interpreted this to be a reminder not eat the meat of a young animal that has yet to be weaned from its mother.

In a kosher home, one set of dishes, silverware, utensils, and pots and pans are used for dairy and another set is for meat. In fact, the kitchen will be divided with cabinets to store dairy items, and likewise for the meat, and there will be separate prep areas. In addition, if one has just eaten a hamburger they must wait a certain amount of time before consuming ice cream so that both are not together in your stomach. Obviously, a cheeseburger would be *treyf*. All of this is done to remember to treat animals humanely.

Keeping kosher has become easier with modern kitchen conveniences like the dishwasher, microwave and the oven, but even they must be cleaned regularly between dairy and meat uses. Symbols on commercially packaged food makes it convenient so buyers know what they can expect to find inside. This can be useful for special dietary restrictions. The ingredients are guaranteed to be what is listed on the package. The following symbols can be found either near the product name or by the list of ingredients. The first, called ou (Union of Orthodox Rabbis) means the contents are pareve. If the letter D follows ou, it means the product is dairy. The other symbols indicate the product is kosher dairy.

When my grandmother lived in Eastern Europe she did not have any new kitchen conveniences or special symbols on packaged food to help her maintain a kosher kitchen, and yet it was not difficult for her to keep kosher. Whether she lived in a Jewish shtetl in Russia or in a mostly Jewish city like Balti, kosher butchers and kosher dairy stores were plentiful.

My mother discussed the preparing for Passover in her chapter of "Life in Romania." Passover is an eight day celebration occuring in the spring. During this time Jews celebrate with a special dinner called a Seder, which means order. At the Seder, Jews retell the story of the biblical Exodus by reading the Hagaddah, (a book that is read at the Seder) along with some special traditional foods.

All of the kosher rules are followed for Passover, with one additional requirement. No *chametz* is allowed. *Chametz* is food that has been allowed to rise or where leavening has occurred. The reason for this is based in the biblical story. When Pharaoh allowed the Israelites to leave Egypt after the tenth plague, they hurriedly did so before the king changed his mind. Their quick departure included removing bread from the ovens before it had a chance to rise. Therefore, to commemorate the rapid flight of the Israelites and their freedom to leave Egypt, Jews do not consume any leavened food.

Leaving agents would include anything made with baking soda, baking powder, or yeast. This includes all baked goods that normally are eaten the rest of the year. In addition, wheat, oats, rye, barley or spilt are not allowed if it comes into contact with water for more than eighteen minutes. More than the allotted time, leavening starts to occur and the food is considered *chametz*.

Instead, Jews eat matzoh, an unleavened bread that looks somewhat like a large flat cracker. Ironically, it is made with flour and water but is baked for eighteen minutes, and no longer. The baking process is halted before the matzoh has a chance to rise. To ensure that this is done correctly, the baking is carefully controlled by those who have been trained. Before the baking commences the ovens, the bowls, and the utensils are scoured. In most cases, there are separate facilities to ensure no contamination.

There are other foods that are forbidden, but it's more of cultural influence rather than law. This includes rice, corn, millet, legumes, peanuts, soybeans, peas, string beans, sesame seed, and poppyseed. Whereas Sephardic Jews will eat these foods, Ashkenazi Jews will not. Therefore, any food found to have cornstarch, for example, is off limits as well.

In order for Jews to be assured the product is suitable for the holiday, a kosher for Passover symbol (*hecshur*) is printed on the outside of the package. The symbol helps the consumer identify what is in the container because it can be deceiving. For instance, some brands of sour cream contain cornstarch which may be a surprise ingredient. That additive to the sour cream would make it not kosher for Passover.

To make sure that the Jewish home is ready for the holiday the entire house is cleaned to make sure that no leavened food or *chametz* is lurking in the back of kitchen cabinets or hiding in the corner of a room. It is not just the kitchen that is cleaned, but the entire home; it's an extreme type of spring cleaning. Everyone in the family is encouraged to help in the process and it becomes a game for the children as they "hunt" for *chametz*. Any non-Kosher for Passover food found in the home is gathered up, covered and stored away so it cannot be touched or seen during the holiday.

My mother wrote how her mother had to clean out the water barrel for Passover. She emptied the barrel, filled it with hot rocks and then poured water over so the steam would clean the inside. It didn't matter that only water was kept in the barrel all year long, it was still cleaned out to make it kosher for Passover. In the same way, with today's modern conveniences, a dishwasher must be run empty at the longest, hottest setting to get it Passover-ready. Each kitchen appliance must go through a rigorous cleaning.

For the eight days of the holiday different dishes, pots and pans, and silverware are used. These items are stored all year and only used for the holiday so they never come in contact with *chametz*.

Getting ready for Passover is a huge undertaking that takes many days. My grandmother had to work very hard to make sure all was done correctly. She didn't have a modern supermarket where Kosher for Passover (KOP) foods were labeled and displayed.

She didn't have disposable plates and plasticware to make it easier for her. But even with all of this work, my mother still described the holiday, as "the delight of the Jewish people."

When my mother had her own household she did not maintain a kosher for Passover home. Working at a full time job made it difficult to do all the preparations. It can take days to get all the cooking and cleaning done. I do remember her cooking and baking. She always made a sponge cake. To make it rise, she folded in stiffly beaten egg whites.

My mother made her own rules for Passover. It was simple. I was forbidden to eat any *chametz*. I remember one time, I had lunch at a Jewish friend's house. We were served a sandwich. At the time I was too young to know better, but when my mother found out she was furious. She never said anything to the other mother, but I knew never to do that again, and as long as I lived in my parents home, I never did.

There are a couple of unintended consequences that came from maintaining the dietary laws. One was it gave the Jewish people an identity and united them. They might have come from different parts of the world, spoke different languages, enjoyed different customs, but the dietary laws were the glue that made them one people. Another was, keeping kosher allowed the Jews, almost always a minority wherever they lived, to survive over several millenia. By keeping kosher, Jews lived a life apart from others. They could not socialize with gentiles because social events usually involved food. Therefore, most interactions between Jews and their non-Jewish neighbors were limited which resulted in reduced intermingling. Intermarriage was rare. While Jews have often been blamed for being clannish, the reason was the commandment for adhering to the dietary laws. This separateness has allowed them to endure while other ancient groups have vanished along the way.

Sherry V. Ostroff

My grandmother's and mother's passport. The words are written in French because it was the language of diplomacy for many years. After World War I English started to transcend French.

The SS Majestic, the largest ship in the world at the time of my mother's sailing, December, 1927.

Second Class Dining Room. My mother held a second class ticket. Her description of where she dined did not match this dining room.

First class dining room. Perhaps this is where my mother dined because she mentioned being seated at
a large round table.

Second class cabin

Epilogue

My mother handed her finished story to me in 1987. I have shared it with a couple of family members, and used it with my students when I wanted to convey to them the importance of seeking out and appreciating their family history. I have also related the highlights to close friends. The usual responses I have received are, first, what an amazing tale, second, how fortunate I was to get the story before it was too late, and last, they wished they had the story of their family. Yes, I know I was lucky, because not only was my mother agreeable to write it all down, but that she was mentally and physically able to do so. It is not lost on me that I possess a priceless document.

Reading it, this last time, has been like a new experience. I am now almost the same age my mother was when she wrote it; and age changes perspective. I have always wanted to do something with her story, and for years I did not know how I would proceed. It just took time to figure it out. Also, by matching up her story with the historical background, has added a new level of understanding. I now know the historical, political and cultural events that were going on all around my mother. She could not control them, but they were shaping her experience and her future, nonetheless.

I was amazed at the accuracy of my mother's story when compared to the available historical data and eyewitness accounts. Her details about the pogrom when the Jews were murdered standing against the wall of a sugar factory did, in fact, occur, just as she said. Her depiction of life in Balti, Romania matches the historical description of the city in the 1920's.

When I first read her story there were two details that puzzled me. The first was the name she gave for where her family lived in Russia. She called it *Keifer Gu Bone.* I knew this had something to do with Kiev, but for years I thought it was a misspelling or the haze of six decades clouded her memory. Then, during my research I came upon *Kiev Gubonia*, which is an administrative division in the vicinity of Kiev, and I realized this is what she meant. The second was HIAS which she mentioned in her chapter on Life in Romania. The HIAS was an organization her mother would visit frequently. In her manuscript she always capitalized the letters, but I had no idea what they stood for and the internet barely existed in 1987. This time it was different. I typed those letters on my computer screen, and sure enough, information about the Hebrew Immigration Assistance Society appeared before my eyes. For years, I thought my mother was mistaken, but in reality she knew exactly what she was talking about all the time.

ORT was an organization that I mentioned briefly in my part of the "Life in Romania" chapter. ORT is a

Jewish organization that provided vocational training mostly to immigrants and refugees like my grandmother. There used to be a chapter of ORT in my hometown and I was president of the chapter for a couple of years. I even wrote an article about ORT for a Jewish Encyclopedia. It completely escaped me when I read my mother's story the first time. When I reread her story, and she mentioned that her mother learned the trade of a milliner, I realized that ORT was responsible. Claiming that you had a skill, like a milliner, on your immigration form would increase your chances of getting in to the United States.

There are patterns in my mother's story that I did not recognize before, but now are clear. My grandmother and especially my mother were extraordinarily lucky; they always seemed to be one step ahead of disaster. My mother was born in the midst of great social and political upheaval where it was not safe to be a Jew. Except for her father, the family was fortunate to flee from the pogroms. My mother was lucky that Shandel escaped with her life when she was beaten, robbed and left for dead while trying to collect money that was due to the family. Then, at the border crossing, it was only by chance there was room in the boat that carried them to Romania. Once there, luck was with them again. They were lucky to have family in Balti which enabled them to move from house to house always one step ahead of being rounded up because they were illegal immigrants. Then, they were able to beat the immigration quota system meant to keep

171

them locked away in Eastern Europe. Although they did not know it at the time, they evaded the greatest danger of all, the Nazi invasion of Europe, when their escape route would have been shut off. Under Nazi occupation their chances of survival, at best, would have been fifty percent, for a mother and dependent child, far worse.

If you would have asked my mother if she was lucky in her life, she would have answered with a resounding, "No." She and her mother had a difficult time even after they came to the United States. Life was not easy for an immigrant even if they had a sponsor and organizations that offered assistance. Pride may force those in need to maintain their silence. My mother and grandmother were often destitute and worried how the next bill would be paid or how to afford a doctor or medication if either got sick. An example of this occurred when my mother was in elementary school, and she needed glasses. Shandel could not afford them, so my mother's teacher generously paid the $2 bill.

But, I still believe my mother was wrong; she was lucky. When they had to flee Russia, my mother was a young child. She had no recollection of what life was like before the pogroms, or what her life could have been without them. Except for losing her father, who she did not remember, she did not realize what was lost. As a child she saw the escape from Russia as a game. Her muddy exploits in Romania were mostly fun and her shipboard experience was mesmerizing. She never had adult worries of needing money for escape, putting food on the table, or immigration quotas. Some might suggest that Shandel was lucky too, but I disagree. My grandmother lost almost everything: her parents, her husband, most of her siblings, her friends, her home, and a way of life. Out of necessity she immigrated to a new country, and at the age of forty, it was more difficult to acclimate herself to her new environment.

***

My mother and Shandel received their passport on December 1, 1927. There was one passport for both of them since my mother was a dependent. They had less than a week to say goodbye to family and friends, unload items they were not taking, pack their bags and bake strudel. Another nine to ten days was needed for travel to Paris and then on to Cherbourg to wait for the tender to take them to their steamship. It must have been breathtaking to see the largest ship in the world come into view, watch it grow larger as they came closer, all the while realizing their dream was about to come true and the long years of waiting and preparation about to end.

The list of second class passengers from the *SS Majestic* was entitled, "List or Manifest of Alien Passengers for the United States Immigration Officer at Port of Arrival." It was dated December 14, 1927, the day of embarkation. My grandmother and mother's names were listed next to each, but my mother's first name was misspelled as Iba. This has since been corrected.

Much information can be found on the manifest. Shandel was classified as a widowed housewife who could read and write Jewish (Yiddish). My mother's occupation was school girl, and interestingly she was identified as able to read and write Romanian. I never heard my mother say anything in Romanian. She only knew a couple of Russian words, but she was fluent in Yiddish. The manifest also listed their last address in Balti which could allow me the opportunity to visit the site someday. However, my mother never had good things to say about Romania, so based on that and knowing what she and my grandmother went through to get out, I doubt I would ever go there. In fact, I think if my mother was still alive she would be quite angry with me for even considering such a trip.

So what happened to my mother and my grandmother once they landed in the United States? Their ship arrived, one day later than expected, on December 21, 1927. It was a chilly, rainless day with a high of 41 degrees. According to the manifest my grandmother had $60 in her pocket when she got off the boat. Money was necessary to pay the landing tax and it showed the custom officials you were not destitute. Both my mother and grandmother were checked off as not being polygamists or anarchists and they were in good health.

It must have been a very emotional greeting when my Aunt Anna met her mother and sister after they disembarked. Except for the occasional pictures mailed to her, Shandel had not seen her eldest child in almost eight years. My mother would not have known her sister; she was a baby when Anna left. According to the manifest Anna was their sponsor, her home was in Brooklyn, and her new last name indicated she was no longer single.

Aunt Anna, fluent in Yiddish, found work as a translator for the creation of a Yiddish encyclopedia. She worked on that project for many years. She lived in Brooklyn for the rest of her life and would occasionally visit us, where I grew up, in Philadelphia. She was extremely short, just over four feet tall, and I use to wonder if she didn't shrink a bit each time I saw her, or maybe it was due to my getting taller. To me, Aunt Anna was a very sweet lady who loved her sister and her sister's family. She never had much money, but was always generous and arrived with a satchel filled with gifts for all of us. I remember my mother yelling at Aunt Anna for spending what little money she had. My mother would tell me to give the gifts back, and I would watch the two sisters argue, each trying to be loving and generous in their own way. However, I did not agree with my mother's way of thinking, I thought it was rude not to accept the gifts that Aunt Anna picked for me and wrapped with

175

such care. Besides, like any other child I loved the surprises she brought.

Anna's husband died before I was born, and about twenty years later she surprised us all and remarried. Her new husband, Sam worked as a typesetter for the *New York Times*. He was a kind and generous man, and was an immigrant as well. Anna and Sam started their relationship as good friends, until one day he was out coat shopping with her. As she was about to make her purchase he told her that he wanted to pay for it, and in fact, if she approved, he wanted to take care of her forever. In that shy and quiet way, which is the kind of man Sam was, he proposed to Aunt Anna and they brought each other much deserved happiness. Sam died about five years after they married, and a couple of years later Anna died on December 29, 1975. She was buried near her mother and brother at Mt. Sharon Cemetery outside of Philadelphia. Because she never had any children there was no one who could take her name, so in 1979 when my daughter Jessica was born, I followed Jewish custom by naming her after a deceased relative. I chose Anne for my daughter's middle name. It is a way to remember Aunt Anna and all she did for saving her family.

At some point after my mother and grandmother lived in New York, they decided to move to California. Their stay was short, they returned east, and made their way to Philadelphia. My Uncle Jack married and he resided in Philadelphia with his family as well. Shandel married two more times, but she survived all of her husbands. Widowed for the last time, she lived with my parents till she passed away on May 23, 1950. I was born three months later, and I have Shandel's name.

***

Shortly after arriving in the United States my mother started public school, but she knew little English. In those days there were no classes or teachers to support a non-English speaker, so the school handled it the only way they knew. My mother was started in the second grade when she should have been in fourth. Luckily, it didn't take long for my mother to pick up the language, and when she was proficient enough she was moved up two grades.

The constant theme in my mother's story is being born at the wrong place and the wrong time. Luckily, she was no longer in the wrong place, but challenging times seemed to follow her. In less than two years, after arriving, the Great Depression descended upon the United States and my mother was forced to drop out of high school to help support her mother. Shandel never learned much English, was in frail health, and could not hold down a job. My mother left in the ninth grade; this was not unusual at that time. In desperate times, children of workable age needed to find employment to help their families. This is what you did, and my mother never regretted what was necessary. She found work in an office.

Like most immigrants of the time, my mother wanted to shed her foreign persona quickly and become a full-fledged American. That was evident in how soon she learned English, and because she was so young she never had an accent. She was no longer known by her Jewish name, Ita or her Russian name, Ducia, but now she was Elaine, with a shortened surname, Pogreb. My mother became a typical American teenager. She went to lots of dances and parties and had many friends and boyfriends. She received several marriage proposals, but accepted only one, from my father, Herman. Against all odds, their relationship started out on a lucky blind date. On Saturday, August 17, 1940 my mother changed her name for the last time to Elaine Vernick.

Their wedding was held at my father's parent's home. There were few details and no surviving photographs. My mother told me that it rained in the morning and then the sun came out before the sunset ceremony. Rain followed by sunshine, my parents told me, was considered good luck. My mother wore a satin gown made by Shandel. I still have her wedding dress, and when my daughter got married a swatch of my mother's gown and mine was sewn into my daughter's. She wore a necklace that was once a piece of jewelry owned by Shandel. Therefore, my daughter walked down the aisle accompanied by three generations. I think that would have pleased my mother.

On August 9, 1944 my mother became an American citizen. She told me that in order to become a citizen you had to live in the United States for at least five years and you were required to take a civics and US history test. She had to fill out paperwork to show her intent, petition the government for citizenship, and provide background information on her country of origin and arrival. Two witnesses were required to attest to my mother's "good moral character" and that she was "disposed to the good order and happiness of the United States." The two witnesses were my father's first cousin Anne, who became a lifelong friend, and his mother Sarah.

My mother loved her new country with a passion and was always proud to call herself an American. But, I cannot imagine how she felt when the murderous pogroms like Kristallnacht began with the rise of Nazism. Was she fearful that somehow, someone might come for her, and she might have to be on the run once again? As she watched the newsreels or read the newspaper I wonder what she thought. Did she realize how fortunate she was to have escaped the lion's den? I can only relate that whenever any show or documentary came on television about the Nazis, she would direct a stream of Yiddish curse words at the screen.

I don't believe she ever got over the fear of her bygone refugee days. One poignant moment, I will never forget, took place on New Year's Day in 1960. The Mummer's Day Parade was marching down Market Street in Philadelphia. It was a frigid day, and after watching the parade from the sidewalk for about thirty minutes, my mother suggested we have lunch inside a warm Horn & Hardart's cafeteria. In order to do so, we had to cross the street. We waited for a break between string bands for our chance. At which point, my mother told me that when she was a little girl living in Romania there were often military parades. If one attempted to even put their foot in the street they were shot. I do not know if she ever witnessed that, but to know about such things must have been traumatic for a child. I think my mother was not only trying to make the point how much better life was here in the United States, but it seemed like she had to remind herself how lucky she was that she was really safe. My mother had to remind herself fairly often.

One unfortunate result of my mother's experience in Russia and escape to the United States was how much of her expanded family was lost forever. If her life would have been uneventful she would have been surrounded by many aunts, uncles and numerous cousins. But by the time she set foot on American soil, she had five remaining blood relatives including Shandel's brother Julius and his son. Julius's son moved to California, and I do not know what happened to Julius. Anna stayed in New

York, so by the time my mother moved to Philadelphia she only had Jack and Shandel. My mother always envied those who were surrounded by a large family. Luckily, my father came from a large household and there were enough aunts, uncles and cousins to start a cousins club that continued to meet throughout her married life. In Romania, my mother and Shandel were often forced to celebrate Passover by themselves. In the United States my mother was able to celebrate the holiday that was "the delight of the Jews," with several dozen relatives she automatically gained once she became a Vernick. The contrast couldn't have been more startling.

My parents were happily married for fifty-six years. My parents were fortunate to find their *bashert*, their soul mate. They lived their entire married life in Philadelphia and were always together. They never went anywhere without each other and when one was in the hospital, the other would stay all day. So it was not surprising when my father passed away on August 16, 1996 that my mother's health took a downturn and she suffered a debilitating stroke two weeks later. She could not live on her own anymore and needed full-time skilled nursing care.

While lying in bed in a Philadelphia nursing home, shortly after she was admitted, my mother asked me where my father was? I froze. I didn't know what to say to her, because he had been gone only two weeks. I was afraid if I told her the truth, she would relive his passing all over again, and she would have another stroke. I opted to say that he was not able to come right now. That was sort of the truth. My mother's request was a sad reminder that she wanted him to be there with her, and could not understand his absence. Either my mother's short term memory was altered by the stroke or she thought it was all a nightmare. Either way, reality was absent, and maybe that was for the best.

My mother, Ita Elaine Pogrebiski Vernick, passed away almost seven months after my father on March 7, 1997. She died in the nursing home very early in the morning before I could get to be with her.

My mother and father are buried next to each other in Mount Lebanon Cemetery in Delaware County, Pennsylvania. They are almost next to my father's parents grave, and within a mile of Aunt Anna, Uncle Jack, and Shandel. There is a lovely Jewish custom of visiting relatives' graves near the time of the Jewish high holidays of Rosh Hashanah (Jewish New Year) and Yom Kippur (Day of Atonement). I remember, when I was a child, going with my mother and father every year. At the time, my father's parents and Aunt Anna were still alive so we only visited Shandel's grave and one other grave close by. It was burial site for Jack's eight year old son. He died tragically in in a freak accident before I was born. On Shandel's granite headstone was her picture encased in an oval glass covering. My mother would hold my hand and tell me about her mother. Sometimes she would cry, but she would always lovingly touch the headstone and kiss her mother's picture. In this way, along with my mother's stories, I learned about the woman I was named for.

Now it is my turn to continue the yearly tradition. Unfortunately, I have many more graves to visit: Aunt Anna, Uncle Jack, Shandel, and my beloved mother and father. There is another ancient Jewish custom that I perform every year when I visit their graves. I place a small rock, rather than flowers, on their headstones. Flowers will wither and die, but the rock will last forever. It not only indicates that I have been there to pay my respects, but it symbolizes that their memory and legacy is with me and my descendants forever.

Sherry V. Ostroff

Page 1 of the manifest. Shandel is on line 4, my mother is on line 5.

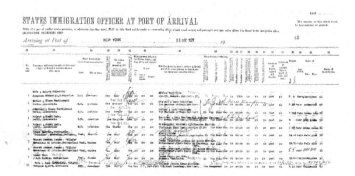

Page 2 of the manifest.

Arrival record No. 3-B-10714

U. S. DEPARTMENT OF LABOR
IMMIGRATION AND NATURALIZATION SERVICE

No. 3   156765

CERTIFICATE OF ARRIVAL

I CERTIFY that the immigration records show that the alien named below arrived at the port, and in the manner shown, and was lawfully admitted to the United States of America for residence.

Name: Ita Pogrebiski
Port of entry: New York, N. Y.
Date: Dec. 21, 1927
Manner of arrival: SS Majestic

I FURTHER CERTIFY that this certificate of arrival is issued under authority of, and in conformity with, the provisions of the Act of June 29, 1906, as amended, solely for the use of the alien herein named and for naturalization purposes.

IN WITNESS WHEREOF, this certificate of arrival is issued

JAN 3 1 1939

er

James L. Houghteling

JAMES L. HOUGHTELING
Commissioner.

... foreign residence was   Priluk, Russia

... to the United States of America from   Sherburg, France

... entry for permanent residence in the United States was at   New York, N. Y.

... the name of   Ita Pogrebiski   on   Dec. 21st, 1927

... S.S. Majestic

... before being admitted to citizenship, renounce absolutely and forever all allegiance and fidelity to any foreign potentate, state, or sovereignty, of whom or of which I may be at the time of admission a citizen or subject; I am not an anarchist; I am not a polygamist nor a believer in the practice of polygamy; and it is my intention in good faith to become a citizen of the United States of America and to reside permanently therein; and I certify that the photograph affixed to the duplicate and triplicate hereof is a likeness of me.

... swear (affirm) that the statements I have made and the intentions I have expressed in this declaration of intention ... by me are true to the best of my knowledge and belief: SO HELP ME GOD.

ITA POGREBISEI — DUCIA POGREBESKY

... subscribed and sworn to before me in the form of oath shown above in the office of the Clerk of said Court, at ...

Philadelphia, Pa.   this   4th   day of   March , anno Domini 19 39. Certification

3-156765   from the Commission of Immigration and Naturalization showing the lawful entry of the declarant ... permanent residence on the date stated above, has been received by me. The photograph affixed to the duplicate and ... is a likeness of the declarant.

[PHOTOGRAPH AND SEAL OF COURT]

(Signed)   George Brodbeck

Clerk of the   U. S. District   Court.

(Signed) By   Harry C. Carter , Deputy Clerk.

U. S. DEPARTMENT OF JUSTICE
IMMIGRATION AND NATURALIZATION SERVICE

This is to certify that the foregoing is a true copy of declaration of intention made by

Ita Pogrebiski — Ducia Pogrebesky

as shown by the records of the Immigration and Naturalization Service. This copy is invalid for all purposes after   March 4th , 1946 , by reason of the expiration of 7 years from the date the original declaration was made.

This copy is issued under authority of section 343(b) of the Nationality Act of 1940, and the seal of the Department of Justice hereunto affixed this   25th   day of

[SEAL]   April , anno Domini 19 44

... and signature of declarant named herein)

U. S. GOVERNMENT PRINTING OFFICE   16—30344-2

Form N-325
DEPARTMENT OF JUSTICE
IMMIGRATION AND NATURALIZATION SERVICE
(Revision of 2-15-46)

APPLICATION No. 3-3-10714   DECLARATION No. 148855

UNITED STATES OF AMERICA

DECLARATION OF INTENTION

_____ of Pennsylvania _____ } ss: _In the_ _____ District _____ Court
_____ District of Penna. _____   of the United States at Philadelphia, Pa.

_____ Ita Pogrebiski _____ (Ducia Pogrebesky)

____ ing at 1125 No. State Street, Phila, Pa.

____ on Office clerk ____, aged 21 ____ years, do declare on oath that my personal description is:

____ female ____; color White ____; complexion Medium ____; color of eyes Brown ____;

____ hair Brown ____; height 5 feet 0 inches; weight 102 pounds; visible distinctive marks

_____ None _____

_____; nationality Russian

____ in Priluka, Russia _____, on March 2nd 1918.

____ married. The name of my wife or husband is _____

___ married on _____ at _____; she or he was

_____ on _____, for permanent residence therein, and now

_____ I have _____ children, and the name, date and place of birth,

____ of residence of each of said children are as follows:

____ not _____ heretofore made a declaration of intention: Number _____, on _____

____ foreign residence was _____ Priluk, Russia _____

____ ed to the United States of America from _____ Sherburg, France

____ d entry for permanent residence in the United States was at _____ New York, N.Y.

____ the name of Ita Pogrebiski _____ on DEC. 21st, 1927

____ vessel S.S. Majestic

____ will, before being admitted to citizenship, renounce absolutely and forever all allegiance and fidelity to any foreign
____ potentate, state, or sovereignty, of whom or of which I may be at the time of admission a citizen or subject; I am not an
____; I am not a polygamist nor a believer in the practice of polygamy; and it is my intention in good faith to become a
____ of the United States of America and to reside permanently therein; and I certify that the photograph affixed to the
____ e and triplicate hereof is a likeness of me.

____ ear (affirm) that the statements I have made and the intentions I have expressed in this declaration of intention
____ ed by me are true to the best of my knowledge and belief: So HELP ME GOD.

ITA POGREBISKI — DUCIA POGREBESKY

____ cribed and sworn to before me in the form of oath shown above in the office of the Clerk of said Court, at _____

____ adelphia, Pa. this 4th day of March _____, anno Domini 19 39. Certification

____-156755 _____ from the Commission of Immigration and Naturalization showing the lawful entry of the declarant
____ ent residence on the date stated above, has been received by me. The photograph affixed to the duplicate and
____ is a likeness of the declarant.

[PHOTOGRAPH AND
SEAL OF COURT]

(Signed) _____ George Brodbeck _____

Clerk of the U. S. District _____ Court.

(Signed) By Harry C. Carter _____, Deputy Clerk.

U. S. DEPARTMENT OF JUSTICE
IMMIGRATION AND NATURALIZATION SERVICE

This is to certify that the foregoing is a true copy of declaration of intention made by _____

Ita Pogrebiski — Ducia Pogrebesky

as shown by the records of the Immigration and Naturalization Service. This copy is invalid for all purposes

after March 4th _____, 1946, by reason of the expiration of 7 years from the date the
original declaration was made.

This copy is issued under authority of section 342(b) of the Nationality Act of 1940, and the seal of the
Department of Justice hereunto affixed this 25th day of
April _____, anno Domini 19 46.

[SEAL]

ASSISTANT COMMISSIONER
FOR NATURALIZATION

____ graph and signature of declarant
(affixed herein)

C. S. GOVERNMENT PRINTING OFFICE   16-31104-2

186

UNITED STATES OF AMERICA

No. 180072

PETITION FOR NATURALIZATION
Under General Provisions of the Nationality Act of 1940 (Public, No. 853, 76th Cong.)]

.... District .... Court of the United States of .... Phila., Pa. ....

for naturalization, hereby made and filed, respectfully shows:

..... and correct name is .... Ita Vernick

..... place of residence is ...1515 Delmont Ave. Apt. 2, Phila., Pa. ..... my occupation is ..... Housewife

..... years old. (3) I was born on .... Mar. 2, 1913 .... in ...Priluka Roumania Russia

..... description is as follows: Sex .. F ..... color ... W ..... complexion .. fair ., color of eyes .. bro ., color of hair .. bro

..... feet ... 0 .... inches, weight 100 lbs ..... visible distinctive marks .. none .... race ...white

..... I am ..... married, the name of my wife or husband is ... Herman Benjamin

..... on .... Aug. 17, 1940 .... at ..... Phila., Pa.

..... Phila., Pa. .... on .... May 29, 1919 .... he resides with me in the United States of

..... with me

certificate No. .... or he/she is citizen by ....

..... names, bar, date and place of birth, and present place of residence of each of said children who is living, are as follows:

..Phila (F) - 10/7/41 - Phila., Pa. - with me

..... was ..... Bucharest Roumania .... (9) I emigrated to the United States from

..Cherbourg France .... (11) My lawful entry for permanent residence in the United States was

..... YORK, NY .... under the name of ..... Ita Pogrebiski

..Dec. 21, 1927 ...... on the .... Majestic

..... certificate of my arrival attached to this petition.

..... lawful entry for permanent residence I have .. not .. been absent from the United States, for a period or periods of 6 months or longer, as follows:

<table>
<tr><td colspan="3">DEPARTED FROM THE UNITED STATES</td><td colspan="3">RETURNED TO THE UNITED STATES</td></tr>
<tr><td>Port</td><td>Date (Month, day, year)</td><td>Vessel or Other Means of Conveyance</td><td>Port</td><td>Date (Month, day, year)</td><td>Vessel or Other Means of Conveyance</td></tr>
<tr><td></td><td></td><td></td><td></td><td></td><td></td></tr>
<tr><td></td><td></td><td></td><td></td><td></td><td></td></tr>
<tr><td></td><td></td><td></td><td></td><td></td><td></td></tr>
</table>

..... to become a citizen of the United States .... Mar. 4, 1939 .... District

..... the United States at .... Phila., Pa. .... (15) It is my intention in good faith to become a

..... United States and to renounce absolutely and forever all allegiance and fidelity to any foreign prince, potentate, state, or sovereignty of which or to ...

..... since the date of this petition, an anarchist; nor a believer in the unlawful damage, injury, or destruction of property, or sabotage, nor a disbeliever in ...

..... organized government; nor a member of or affiliated with any organization or body of persons teaching disbelief in or opposition to organized government ...

..... speak the English language (unless physically unable to do so). (17) I am, and have been during all of the period required by law, attached to the ...

..... Constitution of the United States and well disposed to the good order and happiness of the United States. (18) I have resided continuously in the ...

..... of America for the term of 5 years at least immediately preceding the date of this petition, to wit, since .... Dec. 21, 1927

..... in the State in which this petition is made for the term of 6 months at least immediately preceding the date of this petition, to wit, since

..1928 to 1941 .... (19) I have .. not .. heretofore made petition for naturalization No. ....

..... petition was dismissed or denied by the Court for the following reasons ....

..... and the cause of such dismissal or denial has since been cured or removed.

..... name and made a part of this, my petition for naturalization, are my declaration of intention to become a citizen of the United States (if such declara ...

..... is required by the naturalization law), a certificate of arrival from the Immigration and Naturalization Service of my said lawful entry into the United ...

.... residence (if such certificate of arrival be required by the naturalization law), and the affidavit of at least two verifying witnesses required by law.

..... I, your petitioner for naturalization, pray that I may be admitted a citizen of the United States of America, and that my name be changed to ....

.... Elaine Vernick

..... I, your petitioner, do swear (affirm) that I know the contents of this petition for naturalization subscribed by me, that the same are true to the best of my own ...

..... to matters therein stated to be alleged upon information and belief, and that as to those matters I believe them to be true; and that this petition is ...

..... my full, true name .. SO HELP ME GOD.

Ita Vernick

Above is the signature of the two witnesses. Below is the
Oath of Allegiance that my mother had to recite to become a
US citizen.

188

which she took the advantage well of. So not only did she do ~~work~~ at school at these given subjects but she knew other information that the teacher in her class also did not know about. Her teacher was not very happy to have a student like her, she do always got the best marks, he had to give them to her she learn it. Her marks was always ~~and~~ 80. And she cried bitter tears that with all the answers correct on her tests she never got more than that 80. After a long time she got the ~~an~~ courage together and asked her teacher why he was giving her 80 on a hundred per cent test? His answer was, "Only God knew all the answers it be that gets the 100, the teacher gets 90 & the best student gets 80."

A page from my mother's story. This is in chapter one, the back side of page 14.

189

Aunt Anna in her apartment in Brooklyn.

Shandel outside of my parents' home. She
Americanized her name and was called Jenny.

Elaine Pogreb around 16 years old.

Elaine Vernick as a young wife and mother,
outside her home. Circa 1950

Elaine and Herman Vernick visiting Atlantic City, NJ. Taken
around 1960.

Elaine Vernick in Atlantic City circa 1975

Elaine Vernick with her granddaughter
Jessica Anne. 1981

The Lucky One - Recipes

Fayge's Cookies

This recipe is not my mother's creation. The recipe for Fayge's cookies came from an old family friend; she was also an immigrant. My mother made them fairly often and they became a cherished memory of my youth. She never took credit for the recipe; we always knew them as Fayge's.

I am not sure if I ever met or talked to Fayge, but I do remember when I was fairly young that every once in a while I would answer the phone and a woman would ask for Ducie. I always knew the caller was referring to my mother. These phone calls came till I was about ten, and then they stopped.

Ducie was the nickname for Ducia. My mother hated the nickname because the neighborhood kids would do what kids do, they would make fun of it. They would rhyme Ducie with other words that were not so appealing and would embarrass her. Maybe that was the reason my mother changed her name to Elaine. I guess she figured there was not much they could do with her new name.

I remember my mother making Fayge's cookies. I loved them. She doubled the recipe and made over a hundred. A lot of flour is used to make these cookies and even more is generously sprinkled on

195

the rolling pin, the dough and the rolling mat so the dough does not stick. I remember some of the cookies coming out of the oven with white flour still visible. That did not deter me, I still ate them.

The cookies tasted better once they were cooled, but as a young child I couldn't wait that long. One time my mother had just brought a batch out of the oven and had them on the rack to cool. I asked her if I could have some, but she said not until they were cooled. When she turned her back, I quickly snatched a few, put them in my pants pocket, and quietly ran out the door. I soon realized the hot cookies were burning my leg. The only solution to the problem was to eat the cookies as quickly as I could.

Fayge's cookies are pareve which means they do not contain any dairy or meat products, and therefore if one is keeping kosher, they could be eaten with dairy or meat.

Ingredients:

4 eggs
1-11/2 cups sugar
4 teaspoons baking powder
1 cup vegetable oil
6 + cups of flour

Directions:

Mix the eggs, sugar and oil together. Add the baking powder. Add the flour one cup at a time until the dough appears dry enough to roll out. If more flour is need, add ¼ cup at a time. Dust your mat and rolling pin with lots of flour. Take a handful of dough and roll very thin. Use your favorite cookie cutter. Place on parchment paper and bake at 350 degrees for 12-15 minutes or until cookies are slightly browned around the edges. Recipe makes about 10 dozen cookies. If you prefer a sweeter cookie make it with 1 ½ cups sugar.

The Way My Mother Did It:

I do not know if there was salt or vanilla extract in the original recipe. My mother never salted her desserts (neither do I) and she hated vanilla extract (I like vanilla).

To cut out the cookies, my mother used a drinking glass. She would just invert it, press it down and twist. Her cookies were always perfect circles.

When she rolled out the cookies, she did not have a plastic or vinyl mat. She had a small tablecloth that she only used to roll out dough. This tablecloth would cover the kitchen table. When she was done, she would shake it out in the sink and then pop it in the washing machine so it was clean and ready for the next cooking event.

In later years my mother grew more concerned about making the cookies healthier. She started to use safflower oil because she heard that was more heart healthy.

Varenikis

Vareniki is the Ukrainian word for the Polish Pierogi. I never knew about pierogis till I moved away from my parent's home and saw them in a grocery freezer. To me, they were always varenikis.

When my mother announced she was going to make varenikis I knew that was code for, "Beware! Stay out of the way." But, once she was into a good cooking pattern and the varenikis were moving along nicely, it was a fine time to request a story or two or more: I knew my mother would be a captive in the kitchen for hours.

I remember the trays, one after another, covering every surface of that tiny kitchen and eventually making their way onto the dining room table. You would have thought she was making a meal for an army. While the little half-moons were waiting patiently for their boiling bath my mother would cover the raw varenikis with a clean damp kitchen towel so the dough would not dry out. It was amazing what she could accomplish in her little kitchen.

At the time my mother made the varenikis, I was too little to help. By the time, I was old enough to be of some assistance my mother wasn't making them any longer. The whole process was an all-day affair and very labor intensive. It was too much for her. Her back would hurt her for days after, and my father would beg her not to make them anymore. It was hard for my mother to stop because she knew we loved them so much, and maybe they reminded her of her childhood.

My mother only made them filled with onion and potato. We would eat them while they were still hot. There were always plenty of leftovers. My mother would fry the leftovers.

The potato and onion filling can be used in other recipes. For instance, it's the same filling used in another traditional Jewish dish, knishes. You can make just the filling and have it as a mashed potato side dish.

Potato Filling:

3 ½ cups of potatoes, sliced – If you use golden potatoes you don't have to peel
1 cup minced onion
4 tablespoons of butter

Boil potatoes till soft. In another pot melt the butter over a high heat. Add onions. Stir till the butter and onions are brown. By stirring the bottom of the pan with your spoon you can pick up the browned burned butter and stir it into the onion. Once the onions are a light brown color you are done. Mash potatoes into the onions until they are mostly smooth. The potatoes should take on the color of the onions. Let sit till your dough circles have been created.

Ingredients for dough:

2 cups flour
2 eggs
5 tablespoons of warm water (add more, one tablespoon at a time if you think the dough needs it.)
Small bowl of warm water for pinching dough

Make your dough in your mixture till it forms a ball. Take half out and roll on lightly floured mat. Knead for about 5 minutes. Roll as thin as possible. Because this is an egg dough it will be very tough to roll. You will get quite a workout. Once the dough is rolled out, cut circles using a cookie cutter or inverted glass. Add about 1 heaping tablespoon of potato mixture to the dough circle. Then fold over dough so it is a semi-circle. Dip your fingers into the warm water and then pinch the doughy half circles closed. Use the tines from a fork to help close the dough. It's very important to make sure your dough pockets are securely closed or they will open up in the boiling process.

Drop in boiling water and cook for 5 minutes. With a strainer-spoon take veranikis out of the water, put on a plate and eat immediately with cold sour cream. This makes about 24-30.

Keegel

Keegel is a rice pudding, but it is not pudding in the traditional sense of the way it tastes and looks. It's more solid and can be cut with a knife and eaten with a fork, something you cannot do with traditional pudding. The keegel my mother made was always sweet.

There is also kugel. Kugel is the German word, but it is made with noodles and can be pareve or dairy, sweet or savory.

I always heard my mother call her pudding keegel. It was made with rice, which was available in the Pale, and it was loaded with sugar, cinnamon, eggs and raisins. My mother included lemon zest which is probably something she did when she came to the United States. Tropical fruit was expensive and rare in Romania.

I never knew about kugel until I moved away from home to Lancaster County. Since the area was settled by many Germans, all I heard was kugel, never keegel. Until one day, I was telling a Jewish friend about my mother's keegel. She said her family always called it keegel too. With a little bit of background checking we found out that our ancestors came from about the same area in the Pale of Settlement. Since then I have heard other people mention that their families called it keegel, and again they came from the Pale of Settlement. So, keegel must have been how the dish was pronounced if you came from certain areas of Eastern Europe, and those who came from central Europe called it kugel.

I loved my mother's keegel. It can be eaten warm or cold, but not hot. When the keegel is cooking the whole house smells of cinnamon and sugar and the promise of good things to come.

Ingredients:

1 cup uncooked rice
1 cup sugar
2 eggs - beaten
5 teaspoons cinnamon
1 teaspoon lemon zest
 Butter

Directions:

Cook the rice in boiling water until soft. Drain rice well. Either rinse rice in cool water or let the rice cool. Add eggs, sugar, cinnamon and zest. Mix with a large spoon until all the rice is coated.

In medium size frying pan melt about 2 tablespoons butter over a medium heat. Pour in the rice mixture when the pan is hot. Spread the rice mixture so it evenly covers the entire pan and cook for about 10-15 minutes. Then take the frying pan off of the burner and let it sit for an hour or two until it cools. Then turn the rice pudding onto a large plate. Add 1 to 2 more tablespoons of butter to the pan, get it hot again, and fry up the other side of the keegel. Cook again for 10-15 minutes. Take off of the burner and let cool. Invert on plate. If it doesn't come out easily, then just slice down the middle and take out half at a time. Eat warm or cold. Keep the leftovers covered in the refrigerator. It can last a week, but it won't because it's so good.

This a dairy dish but can easily be made pareve. Use margarine instead of butter.

The Way My Mother Did It

After the rice was cooked, my mother would rinse it under water. She did not like the rice to be sticky and starchy. This also helped to cool down the rice so when she added the egg it doesn't cook it.

The trick to turning the keegel onto a plate, to fry the other side, is to allow it to cool as much as possible. If you turn it while it is still hot it will fall apart. More than anything, good keegel takes time and patience.

As in all of my mother's recipes, she did not add salt, not even to the boiling water.

Sherry V. Ostroff

A Note of Thanks

There are people to thank for this book.

Rabbi Jeffrey Goldberg – For his assistance with Talmud, Torah and all things Jewish.

John Matthews – Always willing to read another chapter and offer his advice, encouragement and friendship.

The Writing Group – Thanks for reading, critiquing and offering suggestions.

A special thanks to my husband who read every chapter and offered his advice. He was also my tech guru and would always come running when I called to clear up another computer glitch. Without his help, I would still be on chapter one.

And of course, my mother and my grandmother Shandel – if it were not for their bravery and perseverance to get out of harm's way, my daughter, my grandchildren and I would not be here today. I am so grateful that my mother was willing to share her story with me. She knew the importance of getting these stories to the younger generation. I believe I have completed what she started long ago in that tiny kitchen.

Sources

Life in Russia:

Green, David B. "This Day in Jewish History/Catherine The Great Tells Jews Where They Can Live." Haaretz.com. December, 23, 2013. http://www.haaretz.com/news/features/this-day-in-jewish-history/.premium-1.564905

Jacobs, Jacob, lyricist. Olshanetsky, Alexander, composer. "Mein Shtetele Beltz." http://kehilalinks.jewishgen.org/balti/mein%20shtetele%20Beltz.htm

Jacobs, Rabbi Louis, "Birthdays and Judaism." http://www.myjewishlearning.com/article/birthdays-and-judaism/

Klier, John. "Pale of Settlement," Yivoencyclopedia.org. http://www.yivoencyclopedia.org/article.aspx/Pale_of_Settlement

Map "The Pale of Settlement." Scale. Jewish Virtual Library. https://www.jewishvirtuallibrary.org/jsource/History/pale.html

Pavlovich, Henry, "Russian-Revolutionary Movements – Jewish Emigration After 1881." http://henrypavlovich.com/Russian-revolutionary-movements-and-Jewish-emigration-after-1881

Petrovsky Shtern, Yohanan. The Golden Age Shtetl: A New History of Jewish Life in East Europe. Princeton University, 2014.

Petrovsky-Shtern, Yohanan. "Military Service in Russia," Yivo Encyclopedia of Jews in Eastern Europe. Yale University Press, 2015. http://www.yivoencyclopedia.org/article.aspx/Military_Service_in_Russia

Rosenthal, Herman, "May Laws," Jewishencyclopedia.com. 2002-11. http://www.jewishencyclopedia.com/articles/10508-may-laws

Rosenthal, Herman. "Pale of Settlement," JewishEncyclopedia.org. 2002. http://www.jewishencyclopedia.com/articles/11862-pale-of-settlement

My Mother's Wedding:

Baumgarten, Jean. "Badkhonim," Yivo Encyclopedia of Jewish Eastern Europe. http://www.yivoencyclopedia.org/article.aspx/Badkhonim

Belder, Alexander. "Names and Naming."
http://www.yivoencyclopedia.org/printarticle.aspx?i
d=2126

"Between Two Worlds – S. Ansky at the Turn of
the Century."
http://web.stanford.edu/group/Ansky/ansky.html

Briskman, Jeffrey and Paul, Jeffrey Mark. "History,
Adoption, and Regulation of Jewish Surnames in
the Russian Empire."
http://www.surnamedna.com/?articles=history-
adoption-and-regulation-of-jewish-surnames-in-the-
russian-empire

Bronner, Leila Leah. "Jewish Hair Through the
Ages."
http://www.bibleandjewishstudies.net/articles/hairc
overing.htm

Freeze, ChaeRanm, 2nd ed. "Shtetl," Jewish Virtual
Library.
https://www.jewishvirtuallibrary.org/jsource/judaica
/ejud_0002_0018_0_18416.html

"Jewish Visual History: The Pale of Settlement"
http://www.jewishvirtuallibrary.org/jsource/History/
pale.html

"Judaism: The Oral Law – Talmud & Mishna,"
https://www.jewishvirtuallibrary.org/jsource/Judais
m/talmud_&_mishna.html

Kirshenblatt-Gimblett, Barbara. "Weddings," Yivo
Encyclopedia of Jewish Eastern Europe.
http://www.yivoencyclopedia.org/
article.aspx/Weddings

"Life in the Pale of Settlement,"
http://litwackfamily.com/the_pale.htm

"Music: Traditional and Instrumental Music," Yivo
Encyclopedia of Jews in Eastern Europe.
http://www.yivoencyclopedia.org/article.aspx/Musi
c/Traditional_and_Instrumental_Music

"Pale of Settlement,"
http://www.simpletoremember.com/articles/a/pale_
of_settlement/

Petrovsky-Shtern, Yohannan. The Golden Age
Shtetl: A New History of Jewish Life in Eastern
Europe. Princeton University Press. NJ. 2014.

Rose, Mike. "History of the Jews in Poland."
http://members.core.com/~mikerose/history.html

Steinlauf, Michael C. "Theater: Yiddish Theater,"
Yivo Institute for Jewish Research."
http://www.yivoencyclopedia.org/article.aspx/Theat
er/Yiddish_Theater

Zollman, Joellyn. "Shtetl in Jewish History and
Memory."
http://www.myjewishlearning.com/article/shtetl-in-
jewish-history-and-memory/

Conditions in Russia – The Pogroms:

Biography.com Editors. "Nicholas II Biography." http://www.biography.com/people/nicholas-ii-21032713 - early-life

"The Czars and the Jews." http://www.simpletoremember.com/articles/a/the_czars_and_the_jews/

Gitelman, Zvi. "Russian Revolution of 1917." https://en.wikipedia.org/wiki/Old_Style_and_New_Style_dates

Heifetz, Elias. "The Slaughter of the Jews in the Ukraine in 1919." http://kehilalinks.jewishgen.org/pogrebishche/History/SlaughterOfTheJews.htm

Goldberg, J. J. "Kishninev 1903: The Birth of A Century." http://www.kishinevpogrom.com/narratives1.html

"Pogrebishchenski," Encyclopedia Judaica. Jerusalem: 1972. Picture of Synagogue in Pogrebishche. https://sites.google.com/site/nachshenhistory/history/shtetlach

"The Pogrom of Zeleny's Unit at Pogrebishche, August 18-21, 1919," Deposition of B. O. Lifschitz. http://www.nachshen.com/lifschitz.htm

Rosenberg, Jennifer. "Balfour Declaration." http://history1900s.about.com/cs/holocaust/p/balfou rdeclare.htm

Tcherikower, Elias. "The Pogroms in the Ukraine in 1919." http://www.berdichev.org/the_pogroms_in_ukraine _in_1919.htm

Trueman, C. N. "First World War Casualties" historylearningsite.co.uk. The History Learning Site, 17 Apr 2015. 28 Oct 2015.

"Self Defense," Jewish Virtual Library. https://www.jewishvirtuallibrary.org/jsource/judaica /ejud_0002_0018_0_17990.html

The Escape:

"Balti," Encyclopedia of Jewish Communities in Romania, Vol. 2. http://www.jewishgen.org/yizkor/pinkas_romania/r om2_00336.html

Hitchins, Keith. "Romanian Democracy," https://faroutliers.wordpress.com/2014/10/6/romani an-democracy-1920s-1930s/

"Jewish Virtual Library." https://www.jewishvirtuallibrary.org/jsource/Holoca ust/killedtable.html

Map for Escape Route from Ukraine to Romania.
http://search.yahoo.com/yhs/search?hspart=ddc&hsi
mp=yhs-
ddc_bd&p=Dneister+river+escape+route+ukraine+t
o+romania&type=bdc-bfr-ai-rhb-
48__alt__ddc_dss_bd_com

Ostroff, Sherry. Jewish American History and
Culture. "ORT," NY: Garland Publishing, 1992.

"The Story of the Jewish Community of Balti."
http://www.yadvashem.org/yv/en/exhibitions/comm
unities/balti/interwar.asp"

Volovici, Leon. 2010. "Romania." YIVO Encyclopedia of Jews in Eastern Europe.
http://www.yivoencyclopedia.org/article.aspx/Ro-
mania

Life in Romania:

"Anti-Semitism,"
http://immigrationtounitedstates.org/350-anti-
semitism.html

"Anti-Semitism in the 1920's and 1930's,"
Abraham Lincoln Brigade Archives.
http://www.alba-valb.org/resources/lessons/jewish-
volunteers-in-the-spanish-civil-war/anti-semitism-
in-the-1920s-and-1930s

"Ellis Island Immigration Timeline."
http://www.shmoop.com/ellis-island-immigration/timeline.html

"Hebrew Immigration Aid Society."
http://www.hias.org/history

History.com Staff. "Knights of Labor," 2009. A&E Networks, http://www.history.com/topics/knights-of-labor

"Jewish Funeral Guide." http://www.jewish-funeral-guide.com/tradition/mourners.htm

Ostroff, Sherry V. "Desertion and the Family: A Study of the Causes and Effects of Male Desertion in Victorian America," Thesis. Millersville University, May 1987.

"Response to Refugee Crises in Europe," HIAS.
http://www.hias.org/faq-hias-response-refugee-crisis-europe

U.S. Department of State, Office of the Historian. "The Immigration Act of 1924 (The Johnson-Reed Act)."
https://history.state.gov/milestones/1921-1936/immigration-act

"What is Cupping Therapy? Uses, Benefits, Side Effects."
http://www.webmd.com/balance/guide/cupping-therapy

"Who Was Shut Out?: Immigration Quotas, 1925–1927," *Statistical Abstract of the United States* (Washington, D.C. Government Printing Office, 1929), 100, chart. http://historymatters.gmu.edu/d/5078/

Coming to America:

Avey, Tori. "What Foods Are Kosher For Passover." 2016. http://toriavey.com/what-foods-are-kosher-for-passover/

Bateman-House, Alison & Fairchild, Amy. " Medical Examination of Immigrants at Ellis Island." AMA Journal of Ethics. Volume 10, Number 4, April, 2008. http://journalofethics.ama-assn.org/2008/04/mhst1-0804.html

"Kashrut, Jewish Dietary Laws," http://www.mechon-mamre.org/jewfaq/kashrut.htm

"Majestic II," http://www.whitestarhistory.com/majestic2

"Vintage Brochure - White Star Line S.S. Majestic: Second Class Accommodations, "http://www.gjenvick.com/HistoricalBrochures/WhiteStarLine/RMS-Majestic/1922/SecondClassAccommodations.html - axzz3uuClNjXD

Author's Information

Sherry V. Ostroff earned a Bachelor of Science in education from Temple University and a Master of Arts in history from Millersville University. She is now retired from teaching in the School District of Lancaster. She happily devotes her time to her writing, her family, including two grandsons, and traveling around the world. She lives with her high school sweetheart in Lancaster County, Pennsylvania. She has no pets at the moment, but she once had a dog named Dog and cat named Meow. You can find out more information about the author and her latest projects at sherryvostroff.com or on Facebook at Sherry V. Ostroff.

CPSIA information can be obtained
at www.ICGtesting.com
Printed in the USA
LVOW01s1503030816
498915LV00017B/784/P